Broken Spring

An American-Israeli reporter's
close-up view of how Egyptians
lost their struggle for freedom

MARK LAVIE

GEFEN PUBLISHING HOUSE

Cover Design: Leah Ben Avraham, Noonim Graphics

ISBN: 978-965-229-668-9

1 3 5 7 9 8 6 4 2

Gefen Publishing House Ltd.
6 Hatzvi Street
Jerusalem 94386, Israel
972-2-538-0247
orders@gefenpublishing.com

Gefen Books
11 Edison Place
Springfield, NJ 07081
516-593-1234
orders@gefenpublishing.com

www.gefenpublishing.com

Printed in Israel

Send for our free catalog

For my wife, Ruth, whose support, strength and love
made this whole adventure possible.

Contents

Preface

After four decades of reporting in the Mideast, I thought I knew the region well. Then Arab Spring erupted as I was working in Egypt. It showed that common assumptions, like these, were wrong:

* The Muslim Brotherhood is an extreme, violent group bent on enforcing strict Islamic law in Egypt and exporting it to neighboring countries.

* Young, Internet-savvy, secular, liberal, pro-democracy Egyptians are Western-oriented and would develop positive relations with the U.S.

* Resolving the Israeli-Palestinian conflict is the key to solving the region's problems.

* When Egypt's military took power, it crushed the newborn democracy.

The trip from such assumptions to reality covers about four years, focusing on the tumultuous years of two popular revolutions and two military coups. I was living in Cairo, walking through its poor, crowded but friendly neighborhoods, shopping alongside my neighbors – learning that Egyptians take their Islam seriously but moderately, much as they live their lives.

They experienced a complete cycle of hated leadership, popular revolution and military coup. Twice.

Egypt's liberal, secular revolutionaries, following the precedent of Tunisia weeks earlier in January 2011, toppled President Hosni Mubarak's heavy-handed twenty-nine-year rule, but they failed to transform themselves into a cohesive political movement to assume leadership of the country. The result was a takeover by Islamist fundamentalists through elections with a thin veneer of democracy.

Some of the same liberal activists pulled off a second revolution, leading to the ousting of President Mohammed Morsi of the Muslim Brotherhood after just one year in office.

By then Egyptians were tired of the constant unrest, which decimated their economy, frightening away tourists and investors. Even the grassroots movement that spurred the popular uprising against Morsi backed the second military takeover after fighting the first one. Attempts to demonstrate against the military's measures to impose order after the second coup attracted only small crowds – a few thousand, compared to the millions who marched before.

Similar patterns have unfolded across the Middle East. In nations where there were popular revolutions, like Tunisia, Libya and Syria, no Western-oriented liberal democracies have emerged, though Tunisia still has possibilities. In other countries, like Saudi Arabia, Jordan and Bahrain, powerful autocratic regimes offered relatively minor reforms to their people to stave off popular uprisings, while imposing some time-honored means of repression to make sure.

Broken Spring takes you into Egypt at ground level. You meet Egyptians, follow their political processes, cringe over their economic deprivation, smile with their innate friendliness, taste the ferment in the region, assess Israel's role – and in the end, begin to grasp why everything went wrong.

The author is a veteran foreign correspondent based in Tel Aviv and Jerusalem since 1972. After covering news events in Egypt starting in 1973, he began reporting from Egypt for longer periods in 2009, moving there in August 2011 for a two-year assignment. As a dual American-Israeli citizen and an Orthodox Jew, he brings that perspective to Arab-Israeli relations through the prism of Egypt, alongside the main theme of Egypt in turmoil.

This second edition of *Broken Spring* adds the perspective of a year of quasi-military rule in Egypt and another war between Israel and Hamas in

Gaza, looking at how journalists like me operate, and cannot operate, in Mideast nations.

Mark Lavie
Rehovot, Israel
August 2014

Acknowledgments

I am forever grateful to my many friends in Cairo who helped me understand their country and their people, to colleagues who explained the intricacies and patiently fielded my many questions, and to officials who spoke to me while trusting that I would keep their names out of print.

I owe a great debt of thanks to Gefen Publishing House of Jerusalem, to publisher Ilan Greenfield for believing in my message and embarking on a solo e-book project for the first time, and to editor Ita Olesker for polishing my sometimes over-simple prose.

And to my long-suffering wife, children and grandchildren, who watched nervously from afar as events turned violent and then calmed, only to turn violent again, who forgave me for dropping in from the airport after all the holiday preparations were already done, even for missing the birth of a granddaughter – I pledge my everlasting love and devotion and promise I'll stay home now.

Introduction, June 2011

On January 25, 2011, millions of Egyptians began demonstrating against President Hosni Mubarak, and just eighteen days later, his three-decade iron-fisted rule was over. It seemed almost too easy. As it turned out, it was. Egypt descended into a cycle of constant revolt, constant demonstrations, constant labor unrest, economic chaos. The signs were apparent at the outset.

Drawing the revolution

Revolution on a wall

"It means freedom," explained the young artist, helping me understand the word that kept appearing in drawings she and her art school classmates were skillfully painting on a wall in a leafy Cairo neighborhood.

Anger is the dominant theme in the row of eight-foot-high wall pictures. Clenched fists. Shouting faces.

The one next to my artist translator's creation is different, simpler. Its two dominant images are a pair of arms, the rope that was shackling them together cut in two – and next to them, two pieces of a puzzle, one with a "2" and the other with a "5." They could fit together, but they stand apart

Egypt's popular revolution began on January 25, so forever it will be known as the January 25th Revolution, though the conclusion came eighteen days later, when President Hosni Mubarak stepped down. Egypt likes to name things after dates in its recent history. The May 15th Bridge runs along and over July 26th Street. Egypt's military overthrew King Farouk on July 26, 1952, and the British mandate in the Middle East ended on May 15, 1948.

The Egypt Mubarak left behind when he quit in disgrace on February 11, 2011, is an overwhelming mess. He's not to blame for all of it, but his twenty-nine-year dictatorship of graft and nepotism did little to overcome the enormous problems this country faces. It arguably made them worse.

Housing conditions make a good starting point. On the outskirts of Cairo are gated communities with mansions that would do Hollywood proud. In the city are slums where families live in hovels around a courtyard with a single toilet. Imagine waiting in line for the bathroom every morning with seventy other people. That is their reality.

Some of those seventy people are employed. Some might sweep office buildings for $300 a month. They're the lucky ones. Some might work in factories for $200 a month. They're the lucky ones. Some could have civil service jobs that pay $100 a month, plus bribes, of course.

They're also lucky.

In the countryside are villages built around factories. Men work seven days a week, make $70 a month, grow some vegetables in their yards and try to subsist.

Yet they, too, are Egypt's lucky ones.

Next to the Nile River is a Cairo neighborhood called Imbaba. An open-air marketplace winds north through the neighborhood, not far from the river. The farther you get into the neighborhood, the worse it looks. Crumbling buildings. Rubble. Trash.

Yet the most striking impression is the men, sitting around tables by the dozens in the middle of the day, nursing a cup of coffee or tea, talking, gossiping, joking. Not working.

So we won't bother with Egypt's unemployment statistics. When the lucky ones earn less than $100 a month, what's the point? But millions don't even earn that.

Out of sight in their mansions, Mubarak's cronies are counting the millions of dollars they've salted away in bank accounts only they can locate, after profiting from sales of government assets at bargain prices, kickbacks from other deals and flat-out bribes from foreign companies.

A key symbolic challenge facing a new Egyptian government is to get its hands on that money. The youth who drove the revolution demand it. Good luck with that.

That's just one of the challenges facing a new Egyptian government, and that's *after* there is a new Egyptian government. Let's not get ahead of ourselves here.

This country is being run by a military council. It rules by decree. We journalists can't get answers to the simplest questions about its policies, because no one even answers the phone over there.

The military has set parliamentary elections for September and presidential elections a month or two later. Then it's back to the barracks.

If that actually happens, it will go against the history of military governments the world over. Rarely has the military anywhere willingly handed power over to the people so quickly – or at all. It's even too quick for some of the reformers. They worry that with no background of democracy, this is too tight a timetable for new parties to organize, field candidates and campaign. Instead, the existing parties are likely to dominate.

Those would be Mubarak's party, which is widely hated, and the Muslim Brotherhood.

Though outlawed for half a century, the Brotherhood has kept itself together as a political movement all these years and is poised to run candidates and campaign in most of Egypt's districts. The nightmare scenario is the Muslim Brotherhood, with its fundamentalist approach to religion and society, emerging as the strongest party, taking over the government and turning Egypt into Iran.

There are worrying signs. Just as the fall of a repressive dictatorship frees the positive, creative spirits, it also unleashes the dark ones. Imbaba was the scene of extremist Salafi Muslims, who follow a branch of Islam so far out that even the Brotherhood disowns them, attacking Coptic Christians and burning down one of their churches over a rumor that a Coptic woman who converted to Islam was being held there. Fifteen people were killed in that clash, one of several targeting Copts, the dominant group among Egypt's Christian minority of 10 percent of the population.

The nightmare image of Egypt being taken over by extremist Islamists is put forward by people, notably Israeli Prime Minister Benjamin Netanyahu, trying to scare other people. It is highly unlikely.

Egypt is a mostly Muslim country that takes its religion seriously. It is also a laid-back society that values its moderation. It spawned a revolutionary movement of young adults, Internet-savvy, politically sophisticated and hungry for progress.

There is no chance that they will agree to trade a dictatorship for a theocracy.

Unless.

There is an old theory in economics called Gresham's Law. It holds that bad money drives out the good.

What if there is a political version of Gresham's Law, that evil politicians drive out the good ones? There is plenty of evidence all over the world of Gresham's Law of Politics in effect.

If that happens in Egypt, that the chaos of the post-Mubarak government building ends up empowering elites, religious fanatics, the corrupt or power-hungry despots, then some will say the January 25th Revolution failed.

They will be wrong.

They call it the January 25th Revolution because that's when it started. They don't call it the February 11th Revolution, as if it ended when Mubarak resigned.

People here are well aware that this is the beginning, that there is much to do, and it appears overwhelming. They seem to be willing to give a fairly elected government a chance to try.

And if the wrong kind of government emerges, the hundreds of thousands of protesters may well be out on the streets again. Even now, there are weekly demonstrations in Cairo's famous Tahrir Square, where the popular revolution centered, demanding more liberalization on the part of the military regime. No one is complacent here.

The task is enormous. It's all in that wall drawing.

Those two arms, the rope holding them together cut. Can they reach up and put the two parts of that puzzle together? The artist understood what's at stake.

"It means freedom," she said.

Chapter 1: Journalists can't tell it all

"This is the Middle East, not the Middle West."

That's a favorite saying of Israeli Prime Minister Benjamin Netanyahu, referring to how things work over here. It's a central theme of this book, and it applies to how journalists have to work in the Mideast – why what you read and what you see is not the whole story, why they can't tell you all need to know.

The recent conflict between Israel and Hamas in Gaza is a good starting point. You saw civilians dying and suffering in Gaza. You saw the destruction by Israel's military.

You're heard from Israel that Hamas was firing rockets from crowded neighborhoods, using helpless Gaza civilians as human shields, forcing them to stay in their neighborhoods in defiance of Israeli warnings to leave.

Israeli military illustration of Hamas rocket launching sites

Why didn't you hear that from Gaza? Often, it's because reporters were afraid to tell you. This is no criticism of the reporters. It's another aspect of the dangers and obstacles facing them when they work in war zones, especially war zones in dictatorships.

In some cases, the one-sided coverage resulted from anti-Israel bias. In others, it was bad journalism – literally covering the story you can easily see above ground, like destruction, misery, death and funerals, instead of digging for the real story, why this is happening and how the powers are operating behind the scenes or underground – again, literally. It's the scourge of twenty-first century "journalism" and its instant deadlines, demands to tweet and blog constantly, get something out there that's more spectacular than the competition, and check the facts later, if at all – added to the cruel cutbacks by news organizations around the world. That means fewer and fewer reporters have to file more and more stories, and file partial reports while they're working. It's impossible. I allow myself the quotation marks around "journalism" because I've been a journalist for half a century (I started young), covering the region since 1972, and I fear my profession is not what it used to be, and not for the better.

So those elements are parts of the reason why you did not get the whole story from Gaza. But the most important element is intimidation of reporters on the ground.

After many of the foreign reporters had left Gaza, the Foreign Press Association, which represents local and foreign correspondents for overseas news outlets in Israel and the Palestinian territories, issued a harsh statement condemning Hamas for "the blatant, incessant, forceful and unorthodox methods employed by the Hamas authorities and their representatives against visiting international journalists in Gaza.... In several cases, foreign reporters working in Gaza have been harassed, threatened or questioned over stories or information they have reported through their news media or by means of social media," the statement complained. "We are also aware that Hamas is trying to put in place a 'vetting' procedure that would, in effect, allow for the blacklisting of specific journalists."

The FPA insisted that news media "are not advocacy organizations and cannot be prevented from reporting by threats or pressure."

Yes, they can. Indirect evidence of that is that it was the FPA that issued the statement, not specific news outlets that experienced the intimidation.

It's nothing new. I've experienced it for decades. Autocratic regimes threaten, attack and jail reporters who write anything critical of those in power. Other reporters get the message and just don't do it.

Bringing this element of the Gaza situation up-to-date entails some real dangers.

This is a saga that can't be told directly in detail. If it is, and if specific reporters are identified here, people will be harmed. Not just the reporters, but their families, too.

But if this isn't told, you'll be harmed. You won't know why you didn't get the whole story.

Let's proceed like this: I will draw on my four decades as a foreign correspondent in this region, telling you how it works, giving some examples – but I will not tell you exactly who is involved, and I may take some steps to cover their tracks. So don't try to figure it out.

This is the main factor, for better or worse, and it's clearly both: News organizations make the safety of their reporters their top priority. Whatever it takes to keep them out of harm's way – that's what is done. I applaud that and I support that, though everyone understands that the policy can be and is exploited by tyrannical regimes to your detriment.

For example, in 2001, a news agency refused to release video it had of Palestinians celebrating the 9/11 attacks in the United States because Palestinian militants threatened the photographer and his family with murder. It was what is called a credible threat. The news agency took considerable heat for its decision to suppress the video but courageously stood by its decision, understandably depriving the world of the visual documentation of an important development.

The drive to protect reporters runs the entire range from serious to silly. Fearing injury to its staffers from rocks thrown by Palestinians and Israeli army gunfire, news organizations imported armored cars to drive around

10

the West Bank and Gaza. They cost a fortune and kept breaking down. Then they allowed reporters and photographers to drive around the West Bank in their own cars – but they had to wear helmets. Plastic bicycle helmets. That's the silly part.

Here's the serious part. A typical news report from Gaza described the destruction, interviewed Gaza civilians who related in heartbreaking detail the deaths of their relatives and loss of their belongings, listed the hardships and travail the people are facing because of the Israeli military operation. Halfway through the long story was a single paragraph that said that Israel claims Hamas fires rockets from civilian areas and so on. That's how they protect themselves from charges that they didn't tell "the other side."

But in fact, they didn't. They didn't report from Gaza about where the Hamas rocket launchers were, where the ammunition was stored, where the openings of the tunnels were – if they mention the tunnels at all, which in this case they didn't.

A reporter for a European news outlet told a friend that he saw Hamas gunmen firing rockets from outside his hotel but he didn't take pictures, because he was certain that if he had, they would have killed him. He told the tale only after he was safely out of Gaza. Apparently his news outlet did not have a permanent local stringer there, or he would not have been able to speak even from the relative safety of Tel Aviv without endangering his stringer.

News agencies, newspapers and TV networks use their local Palestinian stringers to do most of the work on the ground. In this era of cutbacks in my industry, there aren't enough reporters, and those they send in are not fluent in Arabic and don't know their way around.

Besides the budgetary limitations, news organizations often hesitate to send reporters into Gaza at all because of the constant danger, and not from Israeli airstrikes. In 2007, BBC reporter Alan Johnston was kidnapped by Palestinian militants and held for more than three months. Many other foreign journalists were kidnapped there and held for a day or two around that time. There have been no kidnappings recently, but the message was clear – foreigners are fair game. The message was heard and understood. For lack of an alternative, news organizations began to rely more and more on local stringers, giving the regime considerable leverage through intimidation. It's expected that news organizations will deny all this – it's part of the dance.

On many occasions, frightened stringers have pleaded to have their bylines taken off stories. Some have been "evacuated" from Gaza for a time for their own safety, after an article critical of the regime was published or broadcast. Families have been spirited out for a while.

So when the stringer returns home and gets back to work, it's pretty clear how he'll behave. Everyone in the home office knows that and accepts it.

The West Bank, run by the relatively moderate Fatah, is no better than Gaza's Hamas in this regard.

Back in 2000, two Israeli reserve soldiers bumbled their way into Ramallah, where they were lynched and murdered by a mob. The grisly photo of a Palestinian holding up his bloodstained hands proudly from a second-story window after the bodies of the soldiers were thrown out is seared into the memories of Israelis. Yet an Italian TV network felt the need to apologize in public for the fact that there was video of the horrendous event – explaining pitifully that a rival network was responsible, and they would never do anything that could reflect badly on the Palestinian Authority. That was a rare public glimpse into how "journalism" works in such places.

Sometimes even the best are turned. A Palestinian reporter duly relayed an official Palestinian story from an Israeli army roadblock near Ramallah in the West Bank, where a pregnant woman had died while heartless Israeli soldiers had refused to let her go through to the hospital. The reporter went to the hospital, where a doctor confirmed the report. Uneasy, the reporter climbed on foot to the primitive encampment where the woman lived, and there, her husband refuted the whole story. The delay, he said, was getting her to the main road and finding a taxi. Once they got to the roadblock, he said, the soldiers cleared everyone else out of the way and sped them through to the hospital – but it was too late. The reporter then confronted the doctor, who admitted that he lied "for the cause."

A decade or so later, this same reporter, like others, refused to touch a story of a Palestinian whistleblower, appointed by President Mahmoud Abbas himself to find evidence of corruption in the Palestinian Authority. He did his job too well, it seems – he was fired, but not before he said he took with him fourteen boxes of incriminating documents, possibly answering the question of where those billions of dollars and euros of aid to the Palestinians has gone. The official approached several reporters, but no story was done until a local Israeli TV channel broadcast a report, and to the best of my knowledge, no serious examination of the documents has been undertaken.

It could be that over the years, the reporter was won over to the righteousness of the Palestinian cause, refusing to do any stories that reflected badly on his fellow Palestinians.

Or it could be that he realized that if he did such stories, he would be cut off from his sources. Or worse.

In embattled areas and less developed countries, local reporters tend to see themselves as part of the "struggle," like the lying doctor above. The straight-shooting local reporter is like a pearl – hard to find and nearly priceless. In contrast, many shamelessly doctor their reports to reflect kindly on whatever side they're on. One West Bank reporter was fired by a Western outlet after it emerged that she was passing out flyers in support of a boycott against Israel at a news conference.

For as long as I've been dealing with Gaza, local Palestinian reporters have affiliated themselves with the side considered to be the strongest. At first, that was Fatah.

It started changing after the first intifada erupted in 1987, when Hamas emerged as a power. For example, the stringer for two major Western news outlets always managed to get the Hamas statements and leaflets in Gaza before anyone else. The leaflets were a key source of information about the new, radical, violent Islamic group. I figured out why he was always first. Turns out Hamas was giving him the leaflets to translate into English, and then he'd pass them on to his clients.

A particular news outlet always got the suicide bomber videos first. Those were the farewell diatribes recorded by Hamas terrorists about to embark on a mission to blow themselves up in Israel. It emerged that the camera crew that worked for the news outlet was the same one filming the statements.

Those are examples of local reporters choosing sides out of both ideology and self-preservation.

Clearly the abuse of reporters and perversion of journalism is not just a Gaza or West Bank matter. This is the situation all over the region, except for Israel. During my two years in Egypt, I saw some of my colleagues beaten, harassed and arrested. The military-backed Egyptian regime jailed reporters for Al-Jazeera in December, charging them with belonging to or assisting a terrorist organization. Three, including Australian Peter Greste and bureau chief Mohamed Fahmy, a Canadian-Egyptian, have been sentenced to seven to ten years in prison.

Some moves are quieter. A news outlet pulled its photographer out of Saudi Arabia, because the regime would not allow him to take pictures of anything. Local reporters steer very clear of controversial subjects. So one of the most important nations in the Middle East, and arguably the world, is not covered properly, because the regime won't allow it.

We do get some news out of Iran, but local reporters there are pretty much confined to rewriting official news releases and interviewing government officials. Iran gives press credentials sparingly, if at all, and if a reporter is expelled, as many are, his news agency can't replace him. So the choice is, either milquetoast official news or no news at all.

Syria's government and some rebel groups kidnap and kill journalists in the worst case, and severely restrict their movements in the best case. Much of the "news" coming out of Syria is in the form of video clips made by one side or the other. Some are so obviously fake that they are almost humorous – almost, because an obviously staged video of "Syrian soldiers" burying rebels alive is not exactly the stuff of stand-up comedy. Needless to say, local Syrian stringers walk a very careful line, and some just disappear for weeks on end when things get too dicey.

It's like that across the region, and it colors the coverage – what you see and what you hear, or mostly what you don't see or hear. Rarely do we tell you about this. The reason should be obvious. If we're writing about one of those places, we can't very well say, um, we can't bring you the whole story, because, you know, we don't want our local reporter hanging upside down by his heels in a dungeon. Because just writing that could bring about such a result.

That's the main reason that video and pictures seemed to flow freely out of Gaza, but critical elements of the story itself didn't, and neither did all the pictures and video. It gives the impression that the story is being covered, when only part of it is being covered.

And all we can do is keep this in mind – the world does not operate according to our democratic standards of free speech. What we see may not be the whole truth. In fact, you can be sure it isn't.

Then there's Israel. It has the freest, most irreverent press in the region, which, granted, isn't saying much. Israeli newspapers reflect the wide range of political views, and that is wide, indeed. One newspaper clamors for an end to the conflict in Gaza, while next to it on the newsstand is a paper insisting that the operation must continue until Hamas is "utterly destroyed," using a chilling biblical term.

But Israel, you might say, has that frightful and undemocratic military censorship. The military decides what can be printed and what cannot. It's so horrible that most news outlets reporting from Israel feel the need to inform their readers or viewers each time a story is submitted to the censor, whether or not it's been altered as a result.

Censorship can be excused in a nation that's at war, but in the age of instant communications, Israeli censorship has run its course. Not that it's unjustified – it just doesn't work anymore. It's too easy to circumvent the censor and publish anything you want on the Internet.

The fact of censorship probably does Israel more harm than good, precisely because it appears as if the government is controlling news. In practical terms, it doesn't. Censorship applies to military operations in progress, as well as a list of items deemed to be matters of national security. In practice, military operations in progress are live-blogged, live-tweeted and live-broadcast all the time now, and there's nothing the military can do about it, so why continue the effort?

On the other hand, the opposite argument can be made. It's not that Israeli censorship actually limits the news coming out of here. The very fact that it's considered necessary shows how free the news media are.

It's a sharp contrast to the rest of the region, where there's no need for censorship. Brutal intimidation and threats against reporters are so much more effective.

A version of this chapter appeared in TheTower.org magazine.

Chapter 2: Polls don't work here

Imagine running an election campaign without public opinion polls.

For decades, candidates in established democracies have used polls not only to test their support, but also to help decide which issues to emphasize in their campaigns. Many politicians let polls dictate their stands on those issues, and they're accused of "pandering" or tailoring their views to the poll-generated pictures of their voters' latest beliefs, instead of showing true leadership.

Now subtract the poll factor altogether. Candidates would run in the dark. Some would say that would be a good thing, eliminating the "pandering." Others say it would deprive candidates – and officeholders after them – of a key tool to determine what the people want, since, after all, along with leadership, they are supposed to represent the will of their voters.

There's a third possibility, and it emerges in societies like Egypt's.

There are polls everywhere. During an election campaign, newspapers print polls at least once a week, ranking the candidates. Professional groups, local and foreign, conduct polls for their own needs.

What happens if the polls turn out to be wrong? Not only wrong, but way, way off? That's what happens in Egypt. In 2011, the polls showed that veteran politician Amr Moussa was assured a place in the second round of the presidential election that followed the overthrow of dictator Hosni Mubarak.

Yet when Egyptians flocked to polling stations, many of them at local schools, they voted differently.

Here's what happened:

Voting at a Cairo school

If you followed the polls right up to the presidential election, and then you stopped reading the news reports, you'd say Moussa must be the president of Egypt by now.

Three days before the first round of voting, Moussa was polling 32 percent, ten percentage points ahead of his closest rival in a field of thirteen candidates. He was a sure bet to make the two-candidate runoff. The only question was, who would be his opponent?

It was no surprise that Moussa was in the lead. The haughty seventy-five-year-old diplomat, who served as Mubarak's Israel-bashing foreign minister and then intensified that main policy line as head of the Arab League for a decade, was by far the best known of the thirteen. And people naturally vote for the candidates they know.

It didn't work out that way. The top two finishers in the first round were Mohammed Morsi of the Muslim Brotherhood and Ahmed Shafiq, Mubarak's last prime minister. Each received about 25 percent of the vote.

Moussa wasn't third. Third place went to Hamdeen Sabahi, a follower of the destructive domestic policies of national hero Gamal Abdel Nasser in the '50s and '60s. This throwback, incongruously adopted by some, but not enough, of the young Twitterati and Facebookniks who headed the popular revolt against Mubarak, got 21 percent.

And Moussa wasn't even in fourth place. Abdelmoneim Aboulfottoh, a Muslim Brotherhood exile who projected an oil-and-water mix of Muslim fundamentalism and democracy, took fourth place with 17.5 percent.

Moussa finished fifth with just 11 percent of the vote.

So what went wrong?

When polls are that far off, experts usually look at the methodology, the timing and the questions to figure out what went wrong, as I learned from public opinion polling expert Prof. Cleve Wilhoit of Indiana University, now retired, who turned me on to polling pitfalls back in 1968.

The methodology looked pretty sound, as far as the sponsor of the poll, the veteran *Al-Ahram* newspaper, was prepared to tell us – 1,200 personal interviews. A margin of error would have been nice, but as you can see, it didn't really matter.

The timing was good – just three days before the election. It showed Moussa dropping from 40 percent to 32 percent in a week, but nothing like his total collapse on election day.

The poll question was pretty simple: Who's your choice for president?

And there is the problem. It throws into doubt all the poll results you see from this part of the world.

Simple one-question-per-subject polls the world over are based on a key assumption: The respondent will tell the pollster the truth.

That's a fairly good assumption in veteran Western democracies, where people are used to speaking their minds, even encouraged to, with no fear of retribution from the government and its security forces.

It doesn't work in a country like Egypt, or, for that matter, in most other places in the emerging world.

Egypt was emerging from six decades of military rule. The last thirty years, under Mubarak, were especially harsh. Police arrested people for practically no reason. They emerged from prison, if they emerged at all, with signs of torture, physical and mental. The Muslim Brotherhood was a main target. Leaders and members by the thousands disappeared in the Mubarak dungeons.

Fear was the coin of the political realm.

And so, a short year later, a pollster comes to your door, knocks softly, and politely asks you, "So, whom are you voting for in the presidential election?"

You look at the smiling, friendly pollster. You don't even wonder if he's for real. You assume he's a government agent out to trip you up. You quickly assess what answer he's looking for. You figure the safest is the candidate closest to the former regime. That's easy.

"I'm voting for Amr Moussa."

Clearly not everyone did that. Just enough to throw off the poll results totally and completely.

This is no news to professional pollsters. Serious polls are made up of batteries of questions aiming to cross-reference responses enough ways to filter out or counteract the tendency, even in established democracies, to try to please the person in front of you, the one who asked the question.

Here's how it works. A 2014 "Radiolab" podcast told of a group of sociologists who wanted to determine how many people cheat on their spouses in an African country. Obviously, asking the question directly would have produced a false result.

So they divided their subjects into two equal groups on the basis of income, education, age and all the rest. They gave each group three questions and asked them to tell the pollster how many "yes" answers they would give, without disclosing which questions the subjects were answering.

One group got questions like these: Did you have breakfast this morning, have you ever eaten an egg, do you like chocolate? The other group got two of those questions, but the third was, have you ever cheated on your spouse? All the questions but that last one evoke obvious "yes" responses.

Comparing the two by subtracting the percentage of "yes" answers in the second group from the "yes" answers in the first group produces something approaching the actual percentage of people who have cheated on their spouses.

The weekly political campaign polls in newspapers, in Egypt and elsewhere, aren't that careful. They tend to ask that one question – and in this part of the world, the result is often skewed by the fear factor.

There's a historical record of this phenomenon, even in ostensibly Western-style democracies.

In Israel in 1977, pre-election polls showed that as always, the moderate Labor Party was going to win. Labor stalwarts founded the country and ran the only powerful trade union, which also owned the main economic engines. To protect your livelihood, you figured it was a good idea not to rile the Labor Party. Even though Israel has a free and open political system, the polls reflected that fear.

And so imagine the shock when the TV anchor, Haim Yavin, looked straight into the camera on election night in 1977 and said, "So — it's a revolution." Menahem Begin's hard-line party had won.

There are polls being done all the time over here. Their results are covered far and wide in the media. They say they reflect attitudes of the people on practically every issue. Some of them probably do.

But many reflect some people telling the pollster what they think the government wants to hear.

Probably just enough to throw off the results. Just enough.

Chapter 3: The economy is backwards

Morsi was not deposed because of his Islamism. Most Egyptians have no problem with strict Islam. He was deposed because he was a bad president running an incompetent government.

Considering the monumental problems Egypt faces, most of them economic, it's reasonable to ask if any government can run the country effectively. Shortly after Morsi was elected, the U.S. started planning how to deal with the government that would replace him – probably the military. Israel took a more direct route, quietly maintaining the close ties with the Egyptian military that have benefited both nations since they signed their peace treaty in 1979.

Subsidies provide an illustration of Egypt's intractable economic difficulties.

Governments of rich countries make money off gasoline.

Governments of poor countries spend money on gasoline.

We're talking billions of dollars, pounds, shekels, euros. The countries that desperately need the revenues are spending it, and the countries that already have it are raking it in.

Gas for ordinary cars costs $3.80 a gallon in the U.S. on the average. It's about double that in Israel.

In Egypt, you can fill up the tank of your clunker for about $1.75 a gallon.

The difference is subsidies. Citizens of poor countries survive on them.

How poor is Egypt? The World Bank says 40 percent of Egyptians live near or below the international poverty line. That's $2 a day per person, $240 a month for a family of four.

How can anyone make it on that? The answer is, they can't, unless someone helps out.

That someone is usually the government. It helps out by subsidizing basic products, like food and fuel. It's a noble effort to keep people from starving to death. And it eventually pulls the whole economy down with it.

A third of Egypt's badly stretched budget is taken up by subsidies, and two-thirds of the subsidies are for fuel. Subsidies are the largest item in the budget.

It's just the opposite in richer countries. Gas "subsidizes" the government.

In the United States, every gallon of gas you put in your car puts half a dollar, on the average, into government treasuries in the form of taxes.

In Israel, drivers pay $8 or so for a gallon of gas, and fully half of that goes to the government in taxes.

So rich governments are making out like bandits on gasoline.

And all the while, poor ones like Egypt's are bleeding money into gas tanks.

Go out on the street in Cairo, and you'll find that often you can walk faster than the routine traffic jam is moving. A forty-minute drive to the airport late at night can take more than two hours during the day. Horns honk, drivers weave in and out, ignoring the lane lines, which are apparently only for decoration. Pedestrians dodge the traffic to cross six-lane streets, surviving only because most Egyptian drivers, even if they're in a hurry, are innately polite and friendly enough to slow down or even stop to let the poor guys make it across in one piece.

Best of luck, folks

When I first got to Cairo, I started out standing on the curb, looking at the streaming traffic and wondering how I could ever get where I was going. So I'd look for an Egyptian who appeared ready to take the plunge, and I'd walk across right next to him. Even after being in Egypt for four years off and on, often I was still doing do that.

It sometimes seems as if every fifth car is a taxi. They're everywhere, and they're cheap. I would never drive in Egypt, and I didn't need to. Wherever I was, I could stop a taxi within a minute or two and go wherever I wanted in the city for a few bucks.

I see four taxis

So what's wrong with this picture?

Most taxis run on diesel fuel, and the government is paying more than half the price of it. It's subsidized at a rate of 57 percent of the actual cost. Regular gas is subsidized at a rate of "only" 30 to 40 percent.

Not only does this drain the treasury, but also, it leads to distortions. Not to mention killer air pollution.

Egypt's finance minister at the time told his parliament in 2012 that 40 percent of Egypt's heavily subsidized fuel ends up on the black market, where it's sold for a healthy profit. He said a canister of cooking gas, which costs $10 but is sold for 40 cents, often gets resold for several times that – still cheap.

Worse, those who benefit the most from the fuel subsidies are not the very poor. Studies show that the higher a person's income, the more they profit proportionally from fuel subsidies.

An Egyptian expert says the solution is simple – subsidize the poor, not the commodities. In fact, that's what wealthy nations do. They call those subsidies "welfare."

The challenge is how to get there from here.

Cutting out fuel subsidies wouldn't just raise my taxi fare. Everything has a transportation component in its price. A study based on government figures shows that if fuel subsidies were eliminated, that would trigger immediate 30 percent inflation.

In a country where so many people subsist on so little, that would cause starvation. Or food riots. Or both. It has often unfolded that way elsewhere in the emerging world, most recently in Jordan and Nigeria.

But something's got to give. Egypt is running out of foreign currency reserves to buy food and fuel. It applied for loans from sources like the International Monetary Fund. Among the first conditions is – cut those subsidies. Gulf states chimed in with huge amounts of aid, but that isn't a long-term solution.

Subsidies must be brought under control in Egypt. It will happen. It has to. And when it does, it is likely to cause turmoil that will make the Arab Spring revolts of hundreds of thousands clashing with troops in downtown Cairo look like Woodstock.

Egypt's military-backed government headed by "retired" Gen. Abdel Fattah al-Sisi has embarked on a program to drastically cut fuel subsidies, and there have been some protests. So far the security forces have kept them under control, as only a military government can.

Chapter 4: Democracy needs foundations

A clear conclusion emerged from Egypt's various attempts to elect its leaders: Democracy requires much more than elections.

Democracy is one of the world's least understood concepts. Even centuries-old democracies don't really grasp how it has to work, perhaps because it's such an ingrained part of their societies.

Here in Arab Springland, the false assumptions have never been made clearer. In one country after another, opposition groups have overthrown dictators. Then they fail to win elections.

The West should have seen this coming. It has had bitter experiences already.

One of the main goals of the Iraq war appeared to be to install a democratic government. Saddam Hussein, a cruel dictator, was overthrown. Elections were held. A prime minister was selected.

Yet the country has descended into violence and chaos.

Oversimplifying just a bit, the problem is that for the most part, Iraq's people voted their religions, which are indistinguishable from their political beliefs. So Iraq ended up with two main political blocs – Shiite Muslims and Sunni Muslims. That reflects the main split among the population. The Kurdish area got its own autonomous government because, in this constellation of ethnicity-based politics, Kurds could not be ruled by Sunnis or Shiites, or both together.

That's the main result of long years of Western military and political involvement in Iraq, costing the lives of hundreds of thousands.

It should have become clear that the West was in way over its head in Iraq when warring Muslims started blowing up each other's mosques and shrines. In 2006, bombs wrecked the ornate, golden-domed Al-Askari Mosque, a key site for Shiite pilgrimages. It's as if Protestants bombed the Vatican, or Orthodox Jews blew up Reform Judaism's Hebrew Union College.

And now these two branches of Islam sit together in Iraq's parliament and try to govern their nation. The result is constant discord and paralysis, while the country falls apart with daily bombings and shootings, most sectarian in nature. That's what happens when politics centers on religion. Elections become ineffective.

A political scientist would say elections have two roles. The one we know about is choosing a leadership. The one we think about less is uniting the people around the chosen leaders. Without that, what's left is nonstop squabbling or permanent revolution, which bring about the same kind of government and societal paralysis.

Arab Spring has shown us other less-considered aspects of democracy.

In Egypt, social media-savvy twenty-somethings led a mass protest movement that toppled the dictatorship of Hosni Mubarak in less than three weeks. What happened afterwards is a good lesson.

The ruling military called parliamentary elections. Campaigning began. There was the Muslim Brotherhood, more extreme Islamists – and dozens of protest movements. There was reformer Mohammed ElBaradei, Nobel Prize winner, darling of the Western media. He had a small local following. So did each of the other protest groups.

Everyone knows that to win an election, you need more votes than the other guy. Everyone also knows that if you're split into twelve parties and the other guy has two, you're toast.

And toast was served. The well-organized Islamists took 75 percent of the seats in the parliament. The fragmented reformers, marching up and down Tahrir Square instead of uniting and campaigning, got just 9 percent.

Permanent revolution in Cairo's Tahrir Square

An expert explained that even though they are liberal and reform-minded, the protest groups have not learned how to join forces. Only the pure ideology of each group is acceptable to its members, and that spells electoral doom.

It happened again when Egypt elected a president after Mubarak's ouster.

Thirteen candidates ran in the first round. Reformers scattered their votes. Some tried at the last minute to coalesce bizarrely around a follower of Gamal Abdel Nasser, part of the officers' coup that overthrew the hated monarchy in 1952 but then went on to impose populist measures, like splitting up farmland into tiny holdings, that Egypt has yet to recover from.

It didn't work. The two candidates who emerged for the runoff were the Muslim Brotherhood's Morsi, the eventual winner, and Mubarak's last prime minister. Each got only about a quarter of the vote.

That means that half the people voted for others. So if the reformers had put forward a consensus candidate, he probably would have won in a walk.

What we learn from this is that the instinct to band together for political gain is not an instinct at all – it's learned. It's part of a culture. It doesn't come automatically with the calling of elections.

A similar scenario has unfolded in Tunisia, though there are signs now that just as it led Arab Spring, it may be the first to install a moderate elected government. In Libya, the tribes that overthrew Moammar Gadhafi are fighting their own battles and ignoring the feeble central government. Syria is still up for grabs, but already it's clear that the various rebel groups are unable to pull together on anything except their desire to unseat President Bashar Assad. If he falls, violent chaos is almost inevitable, and an Islamist takeover is not out of the question.

All this brings home a number of principles:

• Democracy is a way of life, a culture, not just a system of government.

• Compromise is a key – perhaps the key – component. It is an acquired skill.

• Acceptance of views slightly different from one's own is essential to compromise.

• Once religion enters politics, compromise is impossible. Democracy is impossible. Governance is impossible.

Those principles are relevant for all democracies, not just the foundering attempts in this part of the world.

Chapter 5: Cognitive dissonance

For decades, the term "Muslim Brotherhood" has evoked visions of bearded fundamentalists rampaging through the streets, terrorizing women, herding men into mosques, closing bars, banning Western-style tourism – and when they're done with that, exporting their extreme form of Islam around the world.

When the Muslim Brotherhood emerged as the strongest political power in Egypt, many in the West expected the worst. Israel was practically gleeful in its predictions of violence and doom.

For the most part, though, it didn't happen. Attacks on Egypt's minority Christians increased, but that appeared attributable to the breakdown in law enforcement after the ousting or Mubarak more than the rise of the Brotherhood. Serious Islamic religious enforcement campaigns didn't result from even the most strident statements from Brotherhood leaders. The few examples of "morals police" activity came from movements much more extreme than the Brotherhood.

It's a case of cognitive dissonance.

Psychologists explain that cognitive dissonance is the result of actual events conflicting with long-held beliefs. The mind has a problem with that.

For as long as I can remember, and that's a pretty long time, the Muslim Brotherhood has been depicted as an extremist, fundamentalist, Jew-hating, Israel-hating, women-hating, West-hating, progress-hating gang of violent jihadis.

Then they came to power in Egypt. They won parliamentary elections. Then they won the presidency.

It seemed, based on what we think we know, that Egypt was about to plunge back into the seventh century. There were secular Egyptians, a small minority here, who were happy to crow their concerns about that to any journalist who would listen, and believe me, we were listening.

Cairo's everyday Islam along the Nile

When Morsi took office as president, he pledged to be the president of all Egyptians. He appointed an obscure cabinet minister as his premier, not a member of the Brotherhood. So far, so good.

Until people got a look at the new premier. A beard. Aha. An observant Muslim. Proof, they warned, that Morsi was going to shove his ideology down the people's throats.

The upper house of the parliament, heavily dominated by the Brotherhood in elections after Mubarak was ousted, fired the editors of the state-owned newspapers and replaced them with editors sympathetic to Islamists.

Liberals said aha again, a sign of Brotherhood dictatorship, even though regimes of all types here have always installed editors sympathetic to them.

And then came the first legislative edict by the new Islamist leader of Egypt, after an editor was jailed for allegedly defaming the president. Morsi showed his true colors, his clear intention to impose strict Islamic practice on an unwilling public, his desire to stifle dissent. He ordered that from now on, journalists would not be jailed for their writing before they're put on trial. Aha.

Wait, what? Morsi overturned one of the despotic practices of the deposed regime of Hosni Mubarak, just as he was being vilified by the press for everything he does? Cognitive dissonance.

There's almost no limit to it. In midsummer 2012, there were rolling blackouts across Egypt, because the creaking infrastructure has not kept up with the exponential growth of the population and, folks, it was hot out there. About 40°C (104°F) every day. Then two power plants went on the blink in the hottest of the hot, southern Egypt, blacking out large areas.

Immediately the secular politicians and columnists jumped all over Morsi, blaming him for the failures. The fact that by then he had been in office all of five weeks didn't seem to matter.

What was apparently going over everyone's head is the fact that Morsi was freely elected, and his party took nearly half the seats in the parliament. This was what the people wanted.

"We have four years to make our record," said Mohammed Khatib, age thirty-two, a Brotherhood activist. I had wandered into a local Brotherhood office in an old Cairo apartment building, looking for someone to interview.

The soft-spoken Khatib, clean-shaven, wearing a work shirt and jeans and looking totally ordinary, said the Brotherhood had no intention of imposing anything on anyone. "If the people don't like what we're doing, they will throw us out," he said. "That's democracy."

As events unfolded, it took only one year for the people and the military to pitch them out, but not because of their religious beliefs; rather, because of their heavy-handed incompetence. In the year that followed, calm was restored – partly because the people were fed up with all the turmoil, partly because the Muslim Brotherhood lost much of its standing, and partly because the military-backed government banned demonstrations. Assessing the relative size of the parts is just speculation.

Experts like Steven Emerson of the International Project on Terrorism warned all along that Brotherhood talk of democracy was a smoke screen.

An article on his website, one of many on the subject, quoted a Brotherhood leader as saying the Brotherhood goal is "establishing a righteous and fair ruling system [based on Islamic Sharia law], with all its institutions and associations, including a government evolving into a rightly guided caliphate and mastership of the world."

That includes Israel. Or better put, that excludes Israel.

British author Sadakat Kadri in his 2012 book *Heaven on Earth*, a well written and dispassionate history of Islamic Sharia law, notes matter-of-factly that the existence of Israel is contrary to Islamic law, which requires the whole region to be ruled by Islam. It's that clear.

Brotherhood leaders proclaimed they would never meet with an Israeli. Morsi declared that Egypt would uphold its international agreements, implying maintaining the peace treaty with Israel but not saying the words.

So it looked pretty obvious. Egypt and Israel were going to be enemies, and the Brotherhood would help its Palestinian branch – the violent, militant Hamas – attack Israel and radicalize the Palestinians.

Then there was an incident that involved Israel and Egypt.

In August 2012, Egypt was shocked by a bloody attack by jihadis next to the Israeli border in Sinai that killed sixteen Egyptian soldiers. Egypt's military embarked on a campaign to uproot the extremist Islamists. That involved sending armed forces into Sinai, though the peace treaty with Israel forbids that unless Israel agrees. So Israel quietly allowed reinforcements but objected to anti-aircraft missiles and tanks. The disagreement went public.

Tension rises. Plot thickens. War drums pound.

Except they didn't. Cognitive dissonance.

Morsi's defense minister called Israeli Defense Minister Ehud Barak and told him it's all meant to rein in the jihadis, something Israel wants, too, and it's temporary. So they worked it out.

Does this mean it's all good? Nothing will happen? Not likely.

The Muslim Brotherhood's ideology is unmistakable. Dar al-Islam. It means an Islamic Middle East. That's the Hamas philosophy, too – but with a critical difference.

Though clashes between Brotherhood supporters and the military over the coup were heated, there is no evidence that Egypt's Muslim Brotherhood is prepared to use violence to achieve its religious aims. There is evidence that like the Egyptian people themselves, the Brotherhood is patient, willing to let things run their course. They might be aiming for an Islamic state, but by persuasion, not coercion.

They might accommodate Israel as a pragmatic interim step, as some in Hamas have said they would.

Or they might not.

In any event, we won't know, probably for a long time, because Egypt's military is back in charge, and the Muslim Brotherhood is off the political stage, probably for years.

Chapter 6: Sad pyramid scene

Three years of political turmoil have decimated Egypt's economy and brought hardships to millions. Few places illustrate the hard times more clearly than the pyramids.

One camel, no tourists

The Giza pyramids, the best known of the ancient tombs, are just outside Cairo. Driving there from the center of the city, you don't pass through any empty spaces. At one point you notice that you're in the suburb called Giza. Then you turn left onto a circular road – and there they are.

"It used to take two hours sometimes to get from here to the gate," said Habib, my driver, as we entered. "That was before the revolution." This time we sped right around the large, mostly empty parking area. Habib dropped me off and I bought my ticket. There was no one in line.

First, though, he warned me sternly not to talk to anyone, and not to give my ticket to anyone once I'm inside. "They're desperate," he said.

Even before we got to the site, young men ran alongside Habib's car, asking to be hired as guides. "They can smell tourists," said the soft-spoken driver with a smile, without stopping.

There's a vast plaza in front of the largest pyramid, the tomb of Khufu, also known as Cheops, towering over the desert for more than 4,500 years. If it could tell stories, it would relate the tales of the dynasties of ancient Egypt, its glory and its degradation, its occupation and liberation, right down to the present – the aftermath of the popular revolt that unseated Mubarak in 2011.

If the huge, imposing pyramid were sensitive to noise, it would be feeling pretty good right now. There are very few people to break the silence. The last survivor of the Seven Wonders of the Ancient World is practically abandoned by the modern world.

About a dozen tourists climbed a little way up the pyramid to an artificial entrance. Some went in, others just climbed back down. Nearby, a group of Japanese tourists, a single busload, walked by, following their guide.

That was it.

So no wonder the men hawking souvenirs – little pyramids, Sphinxes, headscarves, postcards, Egypt guidebooks – and men with nothing to sell except themselves ("Here, give me your camera, I'll take your picture") were overeager. There were more of them than there were tourists. As the bus carrying the Japanese pulled up, the crowd of dozens of hawkers converged on the visitors like bees on a hive.

Waiting for tourists

This picture of Habib and me cost me fifty cents.

That's Habib on the right

Later I talked to Mohammed, one of the young men, as he pressed a headdress into my hand. He told me what was obvious – "There are no tourists here, I can't make enough money to feed my family" – and I gave him three dollars for the headdress. He kept asking, almost pleading, for more.

All over Egypt, there are scenes of desperation like this in different configurations. There are no accurate unemployment statistics, but the majority of people here are poor, with little hope for improvement. The situation is only getting worse.

The macro figures almost speak for themselves.

After pouring billions of dollars into the market to prop up the Egyptian pound, Egypt's central bank had to give up when the level of its foreign currency reserves dropped to what it called a "critical" level, enough for just three months of imports, like food. It devised a scheme to control devaluation of the currency, and it lost "only" 7 percent of its value in two weeks. That was just the beginning. Eventually it topped seven pounds to the dollar, reflecting a 15 percent drop in its value.

Crossing the threshold of 7

Foreign investment has dried up along with tourism, for the same reason. Foreigners are frightened about the political instability here.

Egypt elected an Islamist president. Courts dissolved the elected Islamist-dominated parliament. Street riots accompanied the process of drafting and approving a constitution. The people rose up again, and the military ousted the Islamist president.

Whatever the internal reasons, the picture of Egypt presented to the world is unchanged since the uprising – instability, conflict, turmoil – the image that has driven foreign investors and tourists away for the last two years.

In fact, the violence is localized around a few government buildings, a palace and a downtown Cairo square. There is more street crime than before, but before it was almost nonexistent. Though there can be no guarantees anywhere, people who take the obvious precautions are pretty safe here.

Even the hawkers and the camel drivers at the pyramids are relatively polite. If you ask them to leave you alone, eventually they do.

Lonely Sphinx

So if you concluded that this would be a good time to visit Egypt, you'd have the pyramids all to yourself.

Chapter 7: Considerate street walking

The key to understanding how Egyptians cope with their hardships and upheavals is to watch how they treat each other. Also, you could try getting hit by a car.

People walk in the streets here.

There are a few sidewalks. Most are narrow, some blocked with garbage, others lacerated with deep entrances to underground parking that practically require a Bailey bridge to cross.

So walking in the street is often the only option.

Walking in Cairo

That means interacting with Egyptian drivers on an up-close and personal basis.

There is a famous, well-documented psychological theory of driving: The way people drive reflects their true character. Aggressive people drive aggressively, careful people drive carefully, timid people drive timidly. Even those who put on a false public front reveal their true natures behind the wheel.

Before you waste your time Googling this famous, tested and proven theory, I admit it's mine, and the evidence to back it up is only empirical.

So you're picturing walking in the streets of Tel Aviv or New York and wondering how you'd be received by the local drivers. Imagining the curses and one-finger salutes.

Here, streets are not just for driving and walking. They're also for buying and selling.

One of my favorite shopping streets is behind the massive state TV building along the Nile. It's a narrow street, barely enough room for the cars, much less us – and the carts of merchandise that are also in the street. It's where I buy electrical cords, screwdrivers, cotton swabs, a flashlight, even a watch.

Shopping in the street

One day I was walking along and spotted something on the other side of the street. I took a step in that direction, and wham! A slow-moving car (there aren't any other types there) hit me a glancing blow on my leg.

It was totally my fault. I stepped out into the street without looking.

The driver scooted over to roll down the passenger window of his ancient yellow clunker, and I braced myself. Here it comes. I'm about to learn some new, spicy curse words in Arabic.

The thirtyish, bespectacled man leaned to the window and said, "Are you all right, sir?" A worried look on his face, he went on to apologize ten different ways and offered to drive me to a hospital. There was no need, of course, except maybe for my shock at his reaction.

It fits in with the way people treat each other here.

Walking down the sidewalk or the street, a person sees someone coming toward him. Both get out of each other's way. People don't bump into each other. Once, in a crowded market, someone bumped me. I turned, surprised. It's that rare. It was a baby in a back carrier. The baby smiled.

The elevator stops at the ground floor, and someone motions to everybody else to get out first.

And always the smiles. It's the lingua franca.

Walking to work, I got a big smile from a driver when I ducked between two parked cars to let her by. I think she was more than happy to creep behind me until the corner.

It's not just drivers and pedestrians.

I went to the corner hardware store to buy some sandpaper. The shopkeeper didn't have any. So he animatedly gave me directions to a store that does.

I got to the general area, a narrow street lined with simple shops on both sides. I approached one that looked like a possibility and asked for sandpaper. The shopkeeper put a hand on my shoulder and gently directed me across the street and down a bit, while hollering, "Mustafa! Sandpaper!" to his competitor. Smiles all around, of course.

Time for some perspective. There are impolite people here. I sometimes have to dive for safety to avoid cars racing down a narrow street, usually at night, when the teenagers are out. And what I've been writing here applies to men. Women can expect whistles, lewd remarks, groping and worse.

Of course there are many friendly, helpful people in Tel Aviv and New York. As Mark Twain said, "All generalizations are false, including this one."

There are even people here who believe Egyptian politeness goes too far.

Journalist Fatima el-Saadani writes about the concept of "*eib*," literally rudeness. *Eib* is a whole category of frowned-upon acts in Egyptian society, including speaking out against authorities, superiors or elders. It's *eib* even if you agree with the criticism. It's just not done.

This "does not make much sense in post-revolutionary society where many issues and problems still require careful consideration and debate," el-Saadani writes. "These societal norms are a way to scare us into obedience – blind obedience."

On a daily basis, though, it's pleasant here. Whenever I go home to Tel Aviv, I resolve to act more "Egyptian." It usually lasts a day or two. Then people bump me on the sidewalks, clerks snarl – and drivers angrily honk their horns at me.

Just because I'm walking in the street.

Chapter 8: Sex and assault

While we reporters obsess about Egypt's politics and struggles between protesters and the military, and I write about how friendly Egyptians are to me and to each other, there is a much larger and arguably more important scenario playing out every day in every place – routine degradation of women.

The second time I saw Mariam that hot summer day, she was shaking, almost sobbing. Friends were trying to calm her down.

The first time I saw her, she was taking pictures at Cairo's Tahrir Square. I saw her focus on a single orange at a curbside juice stand, amused that, as usual, a non-visual radio reporter (me) failed to understand the visual arts.

Mariam (not her real name) is a young but seasoned news photographer from a neighboring Arab country. Mariam has seen a lot. But nothing like this.

I found out later that between the first time and the second time I saw her, she was sexually assaulted by a gang of young Egyptian men. They surrounded her on Tahrir Square, the symbol of Egypt's progressive revolution, prodding, poking and grabbing her everywhere. Another photographer, a young Arab man, rescued her.

I was off doing what radio reporters do, getting myself into the middle of a street-corner political debate somewhere else on the huge downtown plaza. So I, too, was surrounded by Egyptian men. Mine were friendly.

Of course they were. I'm a guy.

The extent to which women are targets of assault, harassment and just plain bothering here is hard to fathom. Every woman I know, whatever her age, appearance, race, religion or background, has been a target. Every one. It's catcalls in restaurants, whistles and lewd comments on streets – or worse. Much, much worse.

And all the while, I walk around wherever I want with no fears and no concerns. So much so that it's easy for me to forget – and then berate myself for forgetting – that half the people here don't have that luxury.

Before we get started, two caveats: First, these are explanations, not excuses – there is no excuse. Second, female sexual frustration isn't even on the public radar screen. Here, it's all about men. Egypt is still in the antediluvian mode of blaming women for being attacked, as if they bring it on themselves.

Social scientists say that rape is not a matter of sex, it's a matter of power. Here, it's both, and more.

Egypt is described as a "conservative" and "Islamic" society. That means extramarital sex is forbidden. And while it might be nominally forbidden in Western societies, in Egypt there is none of the winking and smiling about it that we know so well. Here, it's actually forbidden. Women are murdered on mere suspicion of affairs. Men must wait until marriage, sometimes until their thirties or later, because they can't get married until they can support a wife.

So sexual repression and frustration spill over.

The same rules have been enforced for more than one thousand years. What's different now is the surrounding environment. Sex is everywhere.

The simple satellite TV package at my Cairo apartment didn't include ESPN, but it did have more than five hundred channels. There were some with Islamic preaching, but many more with Western and Western-style movies and programming. There's an attempt to excise even the mildest of the steamy parts. Movies have innumerable jump cuts from before to after a kiss, and bedroom scenes are cut to the extent that if you don't know the movie plots ahead of time, they can all seem like "What Just Happened?"

Local commercials include the usual sexual elements, but if there is a scene of a man and woman touching, it often includes a shot of the woman's hand sporting a wedding ring. The woman's, not the man's.

If the object is to remove temptation and suggestion from the screen, it obviously doesn't, can't, work. The clear message is that sex is a part of life, but the society doesn't allow it.

Such distortions can lead to hatred and violence, groping, attacking and rape. The causes are male sexual frustration and powerlessness. Every woman here has suffered from it.

What's new is that now women are complaining. Not all, probably not most, but some. It's because women played a leading role in the popular revolution that ousted Mubarak, demonstrating shoulder to shoulder with men. As protests erupted against the Islamist regime that replaced him, that was the case again.

Women demonstrating alongside men

But the cold, hard truth is that despite the mixed demonstrations, the underlying social norms of allowing attacks on women as a matter of routine never changed.

Tahrir Square became the focus of the worst abuse because of an added element: cynical power politics.

Dozens of women have come forward with chilling stories about being surrounded, stripped and abused by gangs of men at the square. It began during the eighteen-day revolt in 2011. The most famous case was the sexual assault on CBS-TV reporter Lara Logan. Her frank report energized other women to speak out.

Even so, it got worse, even systematic. Groups organized to roam the square and protect women against sexual assault. Twitter and Facebook groups were set up as early warning systems, and a website tracked reports of sexual assault in real time with a map.

There were also instances of men forming rings around groups of women to protect them during demonstrations, but then some men would break away and attack the women.

It was clear that many of the worst attacks were orchestrated from above to frighten women away from the square and away from involvement in protest activity. Exactly what that "above" is remains uncertain, because there have been no credible investigations. Suspects include the Muslim Brotherhood, Islamist elements, the police and lingering pro-Mubarak forces.

Whoever they were, they were just tapping into and taking advantage of the underlying issue – sexual harassment and assault as a societal norm. It is everywhere.

One street I walked down at midnight between my office and my apartment is not well lit. One night I was about thirty feet behind two women. I saw a car drive past them and heard the driver holler something. One of the women turned and shouted angrily at the driver as he sped away. It doesn't take much imagination to figure out what had happened.

A few days later, there was a similar setup – two young women walking in front of me. I figured maybe this time I could help out. Though I no longer look like a linebacker, the presence of any male can be a deterrent.

So I stayed about six feet behind the women, close enough to be noticed but not close enough to intrude, I thought.

One of the women turned and looked at me with a worried frown. I smiled.

A minute later, she glanced back again, this time not just worried but clearly frightened.

"It's OK, I'm one of the good guys," I laughed.

She relaxed, her shoulders loosening, her fists unclenching. She smiled and went back to her conversation with her friend.

Did I help? Probably not. The problem is just too big.

Chapter 9: Feeling like a woman

"I've never felt so conscious of being a woman."

That's how my wife, Ruth, summed up her week-long experience in Cairo. She didn't mean it in a positive way.

By then I had been in Egypt off and on for more than three years. I'd noticed and experienced, second-hand, some of the nearly constant harassment women encounter.

I tried to protect Ruth from all that. But I could not shield her from the oppressive reality of just being a woman in a society like this.

Ruth is a sensitive, positive, outgoing person whose first consideration is how she can help others. Her brightness and warmth reflect off people, open them up. They trust her, communicate with her. I know that sounds corny, maybe idealized, but I've been watching her work her magic on people, starting with me, for nearly thirty years now. It's very real.

She was so overwhelmed by her impressions that she couldn't begin to sort them all out until after she got home.

It's not as if she didn't have a good time there. We did the tourist things – the pyramids, the souk, the shopping, the belly dancer. We had drinks at a bar with my work colleagues, coffee with a friend. She enjoyed all of it.

The main object of her trip was to see how I lived and what it's like.

Before she arrived, I drilled into her the necessity to stay next to me to avoid the harassment, to let me carry valuables to avoid purse-snatching, not to extend a hand to a man to shake unless he does first – all the rules that foreigners have to follow here.

Ruth, Mark and friendly Egyptian guy

So she was primed for some of these feelings, as far as men were concerned. Add to that the fact that she lived in Mumbai, India, for three weeks a few years ago, so she's no stranger to foreign customs and third-world conditions. But she clearly wasn't ready for this feeling of female oppression.

At first she thought Egyptians were distant. That's just the opposite of my experience, encountering open, smiling, patient and helpful people all the time – not just to me, the foreigner, but to each other as well – but always adding the caveat that I'm a guy. Given a moment to think about it, at Ruth's urging, I realized that women don't interact with me much at all.

So Ruth was expecting men to be unfriendly, because of my warnings, but by and large they weren't. Her experiences were mixed. Often they paid her no attention, despite her efforts to connect with a smile. On the other hand, young men rose to give her a seat on the train or a bench. She

54

connected with some musicians (she's a singer), and they were friendly. One was a bit too friendly.

What surprised her was that most women would not make eye contact with her. She perceived a mindset of women keeping their heads down, struggling through their day to get to the other side, and if they made it, that was good enough.

By coincidence, Ruth's awareness of FGM was raised just before her visit. If you don't know what that is, please look it up. She found studies that estimated that 90 percent of Egyptian women were subjected to FGM until recent decades, and now the percentage is "down" to 30 to 40 percent. It's widely considered a requirement for marriage.

Ruth found herself walking down the street, passing women and getting upset that every second or third woman she saw might have been deprived of one of life's chief pleasures and fulfillments, instead subjected to physical, mental and spiritual trauma, a condition for finding a husband.

"What are the men afraid of? Comparison?" she observed later, getting to the actual point quicker than most people, as usual. Indeed. Are men in Africa (it's a continent-wide phenomenon not linked to Islam – Christians subject their women to FGM as well) worried that if their women are sexually enabled, they will find other men more attractive than their partners? Good point.

Yet the men, too, are ensnared by the taboos. As we toured the pyramids with a young guide, he made jokes about introducing Ruth to my "Egyptian wife." He said it several times. It was not a language problem – his English was just fine. So I got to thinking afterward about why he joked about my "Egyptian wife" instead of my "Egyptian girlfriend." It's pretty clear. Egyptians don't have girlfriends. They're married or celibate or visit prostitutes. Mostly, they're frustrated.

After the pyramids we endured another Egyptian tourist event – the perfume shop. It's a half-hour presentation where the owner does a whole performance and brings samples of perfumes. While there are one or two for the man, the focus is, of course, on the woman, as it is in the West.

The most special concoction he showed Ruth was called "After Midnight." He presented this as something that would drive her man so wild that they would not sleep after midnight.

So let's get this straight. A woman is subject to FGM, must cover her hair, is forbidden to touch or talk to a man who is not her relative or not her husband – yet it is still her duty to arouse passion in her mate?

That's the atmosphere that my beautiful, sensitive, caring and intelligent wife was taking in. It was so strong that she tried to write about it. It was too much for her. I'm the writer – I'm the one who gets catharsis by putting words down. So this is my attempt to speak for her.

I'm sure it's inadequate. I can never feel like a woman.

Chapter 10: No compromise

There is no word for "compromise" in Arabic. It's a glaring hole in the bucket that's supposed to hold Egypt's democratic aspirations.

A linguist tells me there's a term for "middle position," but that's just a place, not a broad concept like compromise.

That missing factor could propel Egypt toward extended turmoil.

It's well known that language reflects society, and vice versa. If there's no word for something, that concept usually is not part of the culture.

Language reveals much about how people think.

Back in 1972, when I was learning Hebrew from scratch, I was in a class of twenty-six young adults. The teacher had to keep us challenged (as if the right-to-left language with no vowels wasn't challenging enough).

One game she had us play was taking two pieces of paper, writing a question on one and the answer on the other. Then the class had to put the pairs together correctly.

One American jokester wrote "*lama*" on one paper. That means "why." Then he wrote "*ki*" on the other. That means "because." Very funny.

Funnier because when Israeli kids ask "*lama*," the wise-guy answer isn't "*ki*," it's "*kacha*." That means "That's the way it is." A totally different concept. There's no (be)cause as in English. It's just that way. It's a window on the somewhat fatalistic Israeli mind set.

I have yet to figure out why English is the only language I know that doesn't have the equivalent of "bon appétit." "Eat hearty" and "dig in" don't make the grade.

Now about compromise.

It's the key ingredient of democracy. Yet the lack of the ability to compromise is evident all around Egypt.

It has kept the diverse and squabbling opposition groups from uniting. And as crises develop, it has made it impossible to negotiate.

President Morsi, fed up with the courts tripping him up, put himself above the judiciary in a Nov. 22, 2012, decree. He also exempted his constitutional assembly from judicial review so that he could ram a constitution through and call a quick referendum the following two Saturdays.

Secular and liberal Egyptians reacted instantly, pouring into the streets. Cairo cafés filled with young reformers, adrenalin spiking, excited that they were back in the game. They had managed to bring down a president, Hosni Mubarak, but they were unable to make an impact on any of the elections that followed – because they could not unite and work together.

Now they were in the streets again, 200,000 at one demonstration, demanding that Morsi rescind his decrees and postpone the referendum. One argument for the latter was that there was not enough time to study it.

Daily demonstrations

Well, granted, it was a preamble and 236 articles long. It took me nearly an hour to read the whole thing and understand it. Two weeks should have been enough time for anyone to read it and study it. So that wasn't the problem.

The liberals walked out of the constitutional drafting panel because they were outvoted, and because the dominant Islamists did not bend in their direction for the sake of inclusiveness.

Now the liberals wanted to torpedo approval of the constitution any way they could, saying it opened the way to implementation of Sharia law, discrimination against women and all kinds of other sins.

So you'd think the way to get that done would be to go out there and persuade 50 percent of the people plus one to vote no. Instead, the opposition started playing politics. Badly.

Some wanted to boycott the referendum, denying the constitution its "legitimacy." Others claimed a simple majority wouldn't be enough – a constitution has to be a consensus document with a large majority. So some argued for a boycott, and others called for a mass "no" vote. They couldn't agree. Finally they sent out an equivocal call for a "no," but added they still might boycott if their "conditions" aren't met. Not exactly a bugle call to battle.

Meanwhile, Morsi shuffled the deck. He rescinded his decree putting himself above the judiciary and called for talks with the opposition. But the opposition refused. First call off the referendum, then we'll talk, they replied, and boycotted the meeting.

So you see what's going on here. In the absence of a concept of compromise, the way it works is, first give in to all our demands, and then we can talk.

And among themselves, all the opposition groups succeed in doing is bring people out into the streets. They can't forge a unified policy on anything.

It was clear that if they lost, the opposition would declare the results "illegitimate" and refuse to recognize them. That's what happened. The turmoil continued. Morsi asked the Egyptian military to step in and help keep order. Once you let that cat out of the bag, it's hard to stuff it back in, as he found out when the military deposed him seven months later.

Yet legitimacy comes with winning elections. Morsi won an election for president. His Muslim Brotherhood won elections for parliament. Good sense would indicate that the opposition needed to put its head down, work with the elected government if it can and gear up to win the next election. The government should have been eager to work with the opposition, because inclusion is safer, and better politics, than exclusion. There's a famous quote from President Lyndon B. Johnson, that (slightly sanitized) goes, "It's better to have him inside the tent looking out than outside the tent looking in."

Everyone is outside one Egyptian tent or another, because no one can bend principles and join forces with allies, much less rivals. It's because the concept is missing.

Cairo's Al-Azhar is the Sunni Muslim world's most authoritative center of scholarship and religious rulings. Maybe a cleric there can pore over the ancient teachings and derive an Arabic version of "compromise."

Otherwise Egypt's experiment in democracy, like others in the region, is doomed.

Chapter 11: Morsi's gamble on Islam

It was common to believe that Mohammed Morsi was deposed because of the fundamentalist Islamist tenor of his Muslim Brotherhood movement and his Islamist-friendly constitution. Reality shows otherwise.

There's a mosque next door to the apartment building where I lived.

There's another mosque two blocks away. And another four blocks away.

Five times a day, the amplified call to Muslim prayer from thousands of mosques reverberates through Cairo. It's a routine part of life here.

Chances are if the muezzin next door overslept and missed the 5 a.m. call, I'd jerk straight up in bed and scream, "WHAT WASN'T THAT??"

The mosque next door

Islam is such an important part of this society that it's not surprising that President Mohammed Morsi gambled on it.

First Morsi usurped the powers of Egypt's courts. Then he rammed a draft constitution through a representative body to beat a challenge from the courts he usurped. Then he called a quick referendum and got it approved.

He was called a "new Pharaoh" by no less a light than Mohamed ElBaradei, the best known of Egypt's liberal reformers. ElBaradei won a Nobel Peace Prize for his work with the U.N.'s nuclear watchdog agency. Other critics complained that Morsi was no better than the despotic ruler he replaced, Hosni Mubarak. Agreeing with them, 200,000 Egyptians turned out for the biggest demonstration in downtown Cairo since the popular uprising that unseated Mubarak, opposing his proposed constitution.

They warned that the constitution opens the door for Muslim clerics to oversee legislation, limit basic rights like freedom of speech and freedom of religion and turn Egypt into a theocracy. Some called for "Revolution 2.0." Eventually that's exactly what happened, but not primarily because of the Islamist nature of his constitution.

The Morsi constitution approved by the people, similar to the one that replaced it after the military took power, had a preamble of eleven paragraphs, followed by 236 articles. Even so, critics charged, some things were missing.

Despite the fact that Morsi's constitution provided general safeguards for the news media, most of Egypt's independent newspapers, including *Al-Masry Al-Youm*, shut down for a day to protest its lack of a clause explicitly forbidding the arrest of journalists for writing articles unfavorable to the regime. Such an article was not part of the 1971 constitution this one replaced; news media weren't mentioned at all in 1971. This is what was in Morsi's:

Article 48
Freedom of the press, printing, publication and mass media shall be guaranteed. The media

shall be free and independent.... The closure or confiscation of media outlets is prohibited except with a court order.

As far as it goes, that provides protection for the news media, though it's short on specifics. The fact that this clause was inserted in Morsi's constitution, adding a new element that didn't even exist in the previous one, shows how Morsi's opponents were eager to oppose whatever he advocated, regardless of the content.

The most threatening aspect of the Morsi constitution in the eyes of its secular and liberal critics was an opening they saw for clerics to supervise legislation and, in effect, impose Sharia religious law in Egypt. There's a basis for that in Article 4, referring to the top Islamic research and ruling center:

Al-Azhar Senior Scholars are to be consulted in matters pertaining to Islamic law.

And Islamic law gets this place:

Principles of Islamic Sharia are the principal source of legislation.

That was in the previous constitution. Morsi's adds in Article 219:

The principles of Islamic Sharia include general evidence, foundational rules, rules of jurisprudence, and credible sources accepted in Sunni doctrines and by the larger community.

And that's the opening the liberals were worried about. That could be expanded to make Sharia the law in practice, not just a guide, they warned.

But there's also this:

Article 43

Freedom of belief is an inviolable right.... The State shall guarantee the freedom to practice religious rites and to establish places of worship for the divine religions, as regulated by law.

It mentions Islam, Christianity and Judaism – but that led critics to worry about persecution of smaller sects.

They also complained, wrongly, that there was no protection for women, mentioning them only in the framework of the traditional Islamic family. But, in fact, there's this:

Article 33
All citizens are equal before the law. They have equal public rights and duties without discrimination.

And this in the preamble:

Equality and equal opportunities are established for all citizens, men and women, without discrimination or nepotism or preferential treatment, in both rights and duties.

There's more here, much more, than in the U.S. Constitution, which has a preamble and seven articles. Any constitution is just a framework that must be fleshed out by legislation. So the real power center is the president and parliament, or as it has turned out, the military. Whoever controls those controls the tenor of life here. By itself, the constitution doesn't. No constitution does.

That brings us to Morsi and his downfall. The constitution played a role, not as much for what it was, but for what it was perceived to be.

"He's ruining Egypt," sobbed a liberal activist, tears welling up in her eyes, after Morsi put himself above the courts.

It was a sign of the deep divide. Morsi's Egypt is not the activist's Egypt. Morsi was betting that his would prevail.

There have been five elections since the fall of Mubarak. In the first, 77 percent of the people approved a constitutional declaration to partially replace the canceled 1971 document. In the second, the Muslim Brotherhood and more extreme Salafis won three-quarters of the seats in both houses of parliament. In the third, Morsi was elected president. Then his constitution was approved, and after he was deposed, yet another constitution passed a referendum.

Despite the election that installed him legally, the courts tried to keep Morsi from ruling. That started even before he was elected, when the courts disqualified the main Muslim Brotherhood candidate, citing a rule that anyone who served a term in prison cannot run. It's true that the Brotherhood leader was thrown into prison by Mubarak's regime, along with thousands of others, just because he was a member of the Brotherhood. The court also disqualified the main Salafi candidate because his mother might have had an American passport in addition to her Egyptian one. This takes the term "technicality" to a whole new level.

Then the court topped that, dissolving the elected parliament over a technicality regarding election of one-third of the members.

Finally, the court disbanded the body appointed to write the constitution because it was dominated by Islamist parliamentarians. A new one was appointed, with a similar makeup, and the court was about to disband that one, too, when Morsi made his move.

He saw the judges as holdovers from the Mubarak era aiming to thwart his rule by any means. Notably, the revolutionaries who overthrew Mubarak became the best friends of these courts, escalating the concept of "strange bedfellows" to new heights.

Morsi was the first freely elected president in Egypt's seven-thousand-year recorded history. He believed he and his movement had a mandate to rule.

He believed Egypt was ready for moderate Islamism. Moderate, because no one, not even the radical Salafis, advocated suicide bombers, caging women or cutting off the hands of thieves. So he was betting that his constitution would be approved and a pro-Islamist parliament elected, despite the noise made by the liberals.

His assessment was correct. Egypt is indeed a proud, moderate, Islamist nation. But Morsi failed in his actions.

Had he not overplayed his hand, excluding non-Islamists from his regime and ham-handedly trying to suppress dissent while failing to make progress on any of Egypt's daunting economic issues, he might have won his gamble.

Even though gambling is forbidden by the Quran.

Chapter 12: Legitimacy as a weapon

Mohammed Morsi used the term "legitimacy" about three dozen times in his last televised address as Egypt's president: an arm-waving, table-pounding forty-five-minute midnight diatribe defending his right to remain in office.

He insisted his "legitimacy" came from being the democratically elected president of Egypt, and no one had the right to depose him.

مرسي: لا بديل عن الشرعية التي أفرزت

Morsi's last TV rant

Out in Tahrir Square, about a million people begged to differ, using the same term. They screamed that Morsi lost his "legitimacy" by trying to monopolize power, negate the judiciary, take over the legislature, appoint Muslim Brotherhood activists to government posts and the like.

Tahrir Square against Morsi

So why isn't this term "legitimacy," the third word out of everybody's mouth here, part of the lexicon in veteran democracies?

It's the clearest sign that Egypt has no idea what a democracy is.

It's no surprise, since it's been a military dictatorship since the first coup in 1952 overthrew King Farouk.

What happened here since 2011 is a popular uprising that ended in a military coup that deposed President Hosni Mubarak, a failed military government, a failed attempt at democracy, and another popular uprising that ended in a military coup that deposed Morsi.

In June 2011 I wrote about Egypt's revolutionary and domestic state of mind. It predicted the main events pretty much as they unfolded.

Here's the conclusion:

People here are well aware that this is the beginning, that there is much to do. They seem to be willing to give a fairly elected government a chance to try.

And if the wrong kind of government emerges, the hundreds of thousands of protesters may well be out on the streets again.

It seemed like a good thing at the time.

What actually happened was a failed democratic process based on everyone using "legitimacy" as a club to bash opponents.

Here's how it works:

Opponents of Mubarak manage to bring him down. They revel in their success. They utterly fail to put together a cohesive political movement. They keep marching up and down the square as the Muslim Brotherhood, already well entrenched among the people, organizes its political wing and sweeps to a huge victory in parliamentary elections.

Not long after that, the liberals, who won just 9 percent of the seats, start squawking about "legitimacy," charging that the Islamists are ramming through legislation they favor. Um, that's what they were elected to do.

Failing to learn their lesson, the secular and liberal bloc is unable to choose a candidate for president. There are thirteen candidates in the first round, and the liberals split their votes among half a dozen of them. Inevitably, none of them makes it to the runoff, where Morsi and the hated Mubarak's last prime minister face each other. Liberals wave the vaunted "legitimacy" flag again, dither about a boycott and wail that they have no one to vote for.

So only about half the people turned out in the second round. Morsi won with about 52 percent of the vote.

It took no time at all for the liberals to holler "legitimacy," claiming Morsi actually had the support of only 25 percent of the people.

There are key situations in life where "no" means "no." This isn't one of them. A no-vote is not a "no" vote. It just doesn't count. This basic fact was not understood.

The saga goes on and on. Morsi rammed through a constitution that liberals shrieked was pro-Islamist. And no matter that 64 percent voted yes, it had no "legitimacy" – turnout was 32 percent. Maybe somebody boycotted, they claimed.

Morsi appealed to the opposition time and again to meet and discuss their issues. Most of the opposition refused unless Morsi met their demands, the main one of which was to scrap or drastically amend the constitution, the one the people approved. It's a well-known Mideast pattern – give in first, then we'll talk.

I'll stop there. The picture you are getting is the opposite of the one that's usually drawn in the foreign media – a ruthless, radical Islamist juggernaut trampling all over the idealistic, defenseless, Western, young, savvy, social-media liberal opposition.

Morsi and his Brotherhood are no angels. One of the first things the military did after deposing Morsi was to shut down the Brotherhood's TV stations, which were known for spewing the worst kind of filth against liberals, Christians, Shiite Muslims and, of course, Jews. Christians have become targets to an extent that has not been seen for decades. Shiites, hard to find because there are so few of them, are persecuted. Most Jews are already long gone.

It's an example of abuse of power. All sides misused "legitimacy."

In a real democracy, if a party loses an election, it hunkers down, rethinks its policies, seeks allies and devotes its energy to winning the next election.

Here, the opposition brays about "legitimacy" as if it's some kind of self-defining factor that negates election results.

Could there be yet another revolution? Something is likely to erupt, because of Egypt's real problems – unemployment, subsidies, rising prices, poverty – the factors that make it difficult, if not impossible, for anyone to govern this sick, staggering country.

The military's cabinet ministers and technocrats must now deal efficiently with those crucial issues. If they don't, it will mean Egypt's economy will keep circling the drain. If they do, it will cause enormous economic upheavals that could result in street riots.

And in either case, the liberals will be back out in Tahrir Square, brandishing everyone's favorite weapon.

Legitimacy.

Chapter 13: Is Cairo burning?

"Are you crazy?"

I was about to head back to Cairo after one of my infrequent visits home. While I was away from my post in Egypt, a crowd attacked the U.S. Embassy. My friends were pleading with me to stay away.

It's ironic that I was getting that response from people in Israel, which has suffered from the misleading image of "a terrorist on every corner" for as long as I can remember.

Yet I heard it dozens of times during the three weeks when I was home for the Jewish holidays in the fall of 2012. "You can't go back to Cairo, not after that attack on the U.S. Embassy," they argued. "It's too dangerous!"

I gave a stock reply:

"There's nothing to worry about. I'm perfectly safe there. That little riot was just a couple thousand crazy people whipped into a frenzy by their jihadi leaders for a day or two – out of a city of eighteen million."

"You're both exaggerating," laughed a well-placed expert whom I'm not at liberty to identify.

Walking around Cairo after I flew back, I found it looked and felt like the same city I left two days before the attack in Benghazi, Libya, that took the life of the U.S. ambassador, and then the riots at the U.S. Embassy in Cairo and elsewhere.

The people I met were just as friendly, just as laid-back and welcoming as they were before. My Indianapolis Colts T-shirt evoked "Obama good" and thumbs up from a street vendor selling me a flashlight.

Many men wear galabiyas, the floor-length, one-piece garments so common in Egypt and associated with strict Islam, and many women cover their hair. There is no escaping that this is an Islamic society.

The key is to figure out what that means.

At that time a silly, amateurish movie insulting the Prophet Muhammad brought the demons out from the netherworld. It wasn't the first time, and it probably won't be the last.

The Muhammad film riots triggered reactions like this one from British ex-comedian Pat Condell, who releases YouTube tirades against Islam:

"To call these riots infantile and imbecilic is to give them a dignity they don't deserve," he said in his five-minute rant. "They can only be described as Islamic." He went on, "Let me get this straight. We're supposed to show tolerance and respect for a religion that doesn't know the meaning of either word and goes out of its way to prove it every day."

Many have been waiting since September 11, 2001, for moderate Islamists to step up and speak out. Some have been waiting even longer, since the start of Islamist suicide bombings. And many were wondering if there really is such a thing as a moderate Islamist, considering the years-long silence in the face of atrocities perpetrated by their co-religionists. Condell's broadside reflects the widely held conclusion that Islam is a monolithic violence machine.

Then something about the Muhammad film riots and related extremist violence triggered an internal pushback.

In Libya, where the attack that killed Ambassador Chris Stevens and three other Americans was perpetrated by Islamist radicals and unconnected to the Muhammad film, the reaction was violent. After nearly a year of fruitless persuasion of militias to turn over their weapons following the civil war that toppled Moammar Gadhafi, the murder of the ambassador in Benghazi unleashed an armed government assault on the militias. It was a sign that Libya is not prepared to put up with the anarchy or allow jihadis to get a foothold there. That observation has to be tempered by the fact that almost all events in Libya are tribal, not national, and little that goes on there is as it appears, but this was the first time that the government confronted the militias with force.

Denunciation of the latest Islamist violence has come from many high places.

Sheikh Ahmed al-Tayeb, the imam of Cairo's Al-Azhar Mosque, considered the center of Sunni scholarship in the Muslim world, called for peaceful protests and for "spreading (Muhammad's) moderate ideas."

Al-Azhar Mosque

The imam of what's known as the Ground Zero Mosque in New York, Feisal Abdul Rauf, was harsh in his rejection of extremism and violence from any religion.

Writing in the *Daily Beast*, part of *Newsweek* at the time, in a message for the world as well as his followers, he declared, "We certainly must condemn those who believe that taking innocent lives, whether it is suicide bombers exploding in marketplaces or killers of American diplomats in Libya, is somehow endorsed by Islam."

Newspaper columnists around the region rejected the violence. Writing in Egypt's *Al-Shurouq* newspaper, Imad al-Din Hussein went much further, according to this translation by MEMRI:

"We import, mostly from the West, cars, trains, planes.... We import most of what we eat...as well as all kinds of technology and weapons.... We are a nation that contributes nothing to human civilization in the current era. We import the culture of the West, which we call infidel and curse from morning until night."

And this in a country ruled at the time by the Muslim Brotherhood, perceived in much of the West as violent Islam incarnate. Yet Egypt's Muslim Brotherhood President Morsi spoke out against the violence, after a bit of prodding from President Barack Obama, calling it contrary to Islam.

New battle lines are being drawn in this region. On one side are the violent jihadi extremists, like al-Qaida, who tried for years to unseat secular Arab regimes, only to see popular uprisings do that instead. On the other side are Muslims who want to follow their religion quietly, personally, without stirring the hatred of the world against them. That is the Islam of most Egyptians.

This battle has already taken some lives. It is far from over.

After a couple days of deadly ugliness, the violent jihadis went back under their rocks. No doubt they're waiting for another opportunity. Next time, though, they'll have to take into account that the round of riots they organized in September 2012 backfired against them in the Islamic world.

Finally.

Chapter 14: All there is

"Is that all there is?" asked singer Peggy Lee in 1969 in a marvelously cynical song of disappointment over life's major events.

Many Egyptians must be asking the same question. The military is back in charge, despite their two popular uprisings aimed at installing a properly functioning, democratically elected government.

They demonstrated in their hundreds of thousands in 2011 and ousted a hated dictator, Hosni Mubarak. Eventually they realized that what they actually got was a military coup. The military deposed Mubarak under the cover of their demonstrations and held power for a year and a half.

The giddy celebrations after Mubarak's resignation, punctuated by chants, "The people and the military, hand in hand!" lasted just long enough for the military to enrage the young revolutionaries with its brutal tactics. Then it was back to Cairo's Tahrir Square for demonstrations against the military rulers.

I refuse to write "fast forward" here, because I hate that cliché, and anyway, how many of us are old enough to remember reel-to-reel tapes that would spin in a blur on their center posts in fast forward mode?

So let's "move ahead" to 2013. The debate over whether what happened here was a military coup is political, not factual. Of course it was a coup. The military removed Morsi, a democratically elected president. That's the definition of a coup. The only issue is whether the U.S. government can, or wants to, finesse this in some way to keep funneling aid to Egypt – most of which, by the way, is military aid that would reach the actual rulers of the country. In the end, the U.S. suspended some aid. Not the right step, but it could have been worse – it could have taken harsher, even more misguided action against the military, which is the only strong, stable element in this country and has been the cornerstone of U.S.-Egypt relations for decades.

So with the second coup, history has repeated itself. But not really.

Despite the old saying, history does not repeat itself. Timelines are not linear. Things shift to new planes. The Egyptian people are not the same. To quote an even older song, this one from the 1957 play *The Music Man*, they are sadder but wiser.

On a wall next to a Cairo art school, students express themselves in paintings and creations. In 2011, the wall was covered with a row of simplistic revolutionary drawings. Fists were raised, teeth were bared.

Revolutionary art in the beginning

Now the same wall features classic Egyptian themes, in intricate mosaics.

Art without revolution

As in the art, the scene in Egypt today is more complex than it was in 2011.

During the uprising against Mubarak, people were united. Even the Muslim Brotherhood took a limited role. The trouble started once the revolution part was over. Then the Brotherhood asserted its authority and experience, and the opposition splintered into dozens of uncompromising pieces. No one agreed to talk to anyone else, while the Brotherhood did whatever it wanted.

When the people had enough of the Brotherhood and its president, Mohammed Morsi, they hit the streets again, in their millions. They forced the military to move against Morsi. Well, "forced" might be a bit strong, since the military never had a great feeling of affection for Morsi — not because he is from the Muslim Brotherhood, but because he isn't one of them. He was the first civilian president this country ever had. The others all came from the military.

The Egyptian military is much more than armed forces. It's a bit like the old Histadrut labor union in Israel. It controls significant parts of the economy, valuable real estate, industries and more. There are military bases in Egyptian cities, and soldiers are a common sight.

One of the military's permanent goals is to protect its favored status. It will do whatever it has to. For decades, pulling strings from behind the scenery was enough. Now it has moved to the front of the stage for the second time in a year.

This time it took less than two weeks for the liberal activists to understand what they had done. Instead of a neat Morsi resignation and a quick election to replace him, they got the military again. Sure, the generals appointed a judge as interim president, but there are fewer illusions now.

Some of the groups that demonstrated to oust Morsi started planning to demonstrate again — against the military. They've seen what the military is prepared to do, killing more than fifty Brotherhood protesters outside a base in Cairo. There was quickly a Twitter hashtag that didn't exactly say #forkscaf, a reference to the Supreme Council of the Armed Forces, which is in charge. Again.

More than one thousand protesters were killed in clashes with security forces in the months that followed the second military takeover. Most were Morsi supporters. The dejected liberals stayed off the streets. Their main movement even backed the military-run government.

By now some lessons are becoming clear. The democracy experiment failed because of faults on both sides. The people elected an Islamist president but did not let him rule. The Islamist president made things worse by using his majority to force his Muslim Brotherhood ways on the rest of the people. Not willing to wait until the end of his term, and already demonstrably unable to win an election anyway because of internal squabbling, the opposition did the only thing it does well – it called the people out into the streets.

And it got another military coup for its efforts.

Now the liberal opposition is sidelined, irrelevant, as the military battles with the Brotherhood. It could be bloody, it could be long, but the outcome is not in doubt.

Of course there will be another election or two. That is not likely to change much, because by now it's pretty clear who runs this show. Al-Sisi won election to the presidency with 97 percent of the vote, a result reminiscent of Soviet Russia and Syria and a clear indication of what Egypt's people want now – peace and quiet.

Demonstrations, debates, elections, whatever. Every road to power eventually leads back to the military.

So it would not be surprising if disgruntled Egyptian liberals and revolutionaries were sitting in cafés, puffing water pipes and singing Peggy Lee's old song.

Because now they know. When it comes to power in Egypt, the military is all there is.

Chapter 15: Arab Spring and winter

It is a law of nature that summer follows spring.

Except here in the Middle East.

Arab Spring began with a popular uprising in Tunisia. The wave quickly spread across the region, engulfing Egypt, Libya, Syria, Yemen, Jordan, Kuwait and Bahrain. Even solidly entrenched regimes like Saudi Arabia have been forced to take notice.

The hope in those heady days in 2011 was that democratic, free regimes would replace the despots who had ruled over their peoples for decades with brutality, corruption and mind-numbing poverty.

Reality has painted a different picture. Here is a sample of headlines from the 2012 year-end edition of *Al-Ahram*, Egypt's leading newspaper:

(Egypt:) Reconcile or Bust

Troubled Times for Iraq

Sudan's Sad Year

Lebanon Still Languishing

(Egypt) Could Become Greece

No Algerian Spring

Deaf Ears in Yemen

Bleeding Syria to Death

What went wrong?

Though that question is at the base of much of the tsk-tsking and hand-wringing over how things have turned out in the Mideast, the question itself is misguided.

The notion that a region made up of disparate countries, some with artificial colonial-era borders, could throw off decades of dictatorship and magically transform itself into a league of Jeffersonian democracies, living at peace within themselves and with each other, waltzing into the Western world, speaking fluent English, and taking their places at tables set with fine linens, four forks, three knives and five spoons, and bewigged, white-gloved waiters serving from the left and clearing from the right, is as absurd as it sounds.

Nice hat, but no fine linens

Let's look some of these countries individually.

Syria has been ruled by a minority sect, the Alawites, through the Assad father and son team, for four decades. Others were repressed, especially the Islamists. Up to now the opposition forces have been pulling in all directions. They have never been in power. They did not know how to join forces. They have even been fighting each other. Meanwhile, Assad brutally hangs on, bombing his own people from the air as the world tries to extract his chemical weapons, and various Islamic extremists move into the fray.

Libya is an artificial country. It is at least three distinct entities, glued into a unit by colonial powers. For four decades, Moammar Gadhafi held it together by guile and cruelty. He's gone, and so is the glue. Tribes have taken over. The East has declared autonomy from the West, where the capital, Tripoli, is located. In the south, African tribes are fighting Arab tribes. No one pays much attention to the central government.

Jordan has been the scene of unprecedented demonstrations against the king. Up to now the monarchy, despite its bland, pro-Western appearance, has kept a tight lid on dissent, especially from Islamists (as elsewhere), but unrest over economic hardship is beginning to boil over. King Abdullah II is not the beloved figure his father, King Hussein, was, lacking the charisma and the class his father showed the world. Who can forget how King Hussein came to Israel personally to console the families of seven schoolgirls killed by a deranged Jordanian soldier in 1997, visiting each family in turn, holding the hands of bereaved mothers?

Yemen, the poorest country in the Arab world, emerges as the most stable after the ouster of a longtime dictator. The new leader has embarked on a U.S.-aided battle against al-Qaida militants who took over parts of Yemen's south while the former regime played politics. The transition in Yemen was easier than in some other places, because the new leader was not elected. He took over in a U.S.-Saudi power transfer deal.

Not elected. If we learn anything from the past two years, it's that elections do not necessarily solve problems or usher in the era of those waiters at that fancy dinner table.

There is little tradition of democracy in this region, and the only Arab country where there is, **Lebanon**, implements it along strictly religious lines. Muslims vote for Muslims, Christians vote for Christians. A formal power-sharing plan dictates that a Christian will be president and a Muslim will be prime minister. It's not the kind of democracy the West knows and loves. Even that, under influence of the Syrian war next door and the strengthening Islamic extremist forces there, is in danger.

What we see is that elected governments do not automatically, or magically, have the ability to solve deep-seated problems decades in the making.

Iraq is an example of how imposed democracy can go wrong. The nation is divided among Sunni and Shiite Muslims and Kurds. Each has its own political wing. Iraqis vote for their ethnic groups. The result is stalemate, abuse of power to target rival groups, violence and chaos.

And finally, **Egypt**. On the surface, it looks like the one with the most potential. A Western-oriented despot ruled for decades, the nation is close to homogeneous – almost entirely Sunni Muslims with just a tiny Shiite minority and 10 percent Coptic Christians – and it has a peace treaty with Israel.

Egypt's voters installed an Islamist regime, but the military deposed it after a year of incompetence and turmoil. Egypt's collapsing economy may well make future elections and governments all but irrelevant as the military entrenches its control.

So summer has not followed the Arab Spring – only a long, cold, difficult winter. Both the short-term and long-term forecasts indicate stormy weather ahead.

Then, the optimists say, a new form of government may emerge here, one that's better suited to Mideast societies and peoples than the exported Western model. So stay tuned. This should get interesting.

Chapter 16: No aid to Syrian rebels

Among the perspectives one gets just by reporting from Cairo is a clear view of other conflicts and revolts in the region, from a Mideast perspective. The bloody, long Syria civil war is a key one.

At Cairo airport before flying home, I notice the departure board. It lists Tel Aviv, but not Damascus.

Waiting at the gate, I hear announcements of EgyptAir flights to all kinds of places – Beirut, Casablanca, Abu Dhabi – but not Damascus.

Not to Damascus.

Cairo Airport departure board

In 1958, in the days of legendary ruler Gamal Abdel Nasser, Egypt and Syria joined up in a state called the United Arab Republic. It lasted less than four years, but it shows how close these countries have been historically.

Now Egypt's national airline doesn't fly there. Neither does anyone else.

Damascus International Airport is pretty much shut down. Fighting between the forces of President Bashar Assad and the rebels trying to bring him down is close to the airport, about fifteen miles outside the capital, and airlines won't take the risk of flying in.

Even envoys and citizens from Russia, Assad's main ally, drive from Damascus to Beirut and use the Lebanese airport to fly home.

The civil war has been tearing Syria apart for three years now. More than 130,000 people have been killed on both sides – just an estimate, since the UN gave up trying to count in January 2014 – making it by far the bloodiest of the Arab Spring uprisings. Though there can always be surprises, it doesn't look like the war will end any time soon.

The people are suffering. More than one million Syrians have fled the fighting to bordering nations. In the winter, many cower in freezing, primitive tent camps in Jordan and Turkey. The same camps are steamy hellholes in summer.

Several million other Syrian civilians have become internal refugees, driven from their homes but still inside Syria, somewhere.

The war drags on. Assad's air force bombs towns and cities where the rebels are in control. The rebels shell towns and cities controlled by the regime. Rival Islamic forces, one more extreme than the other, battle each other and everyone else. Just as in other Arab Spring uprisings, Syria's conflict is not a matter of good guys against bad guys.

The misconception about the qualities of the two sides is a factor in a larger equation: The farther away you get geographically from the civil war, the simpler it looks.

From, say, Washington, the Syrian civil war looks like young, idealistic rebels fighting to overthrow a repressive, cruel regime. So some are saying the West, and especially the U.S., should weigh in on the side of the rebels, arm them, help them, even blast Assad's forces with cruise missiles. Among those saying that are U.S. Senators and other powerful people.

It looks different from here.

One day a car bomb blew up a bus stop in Damascus and killed fifty-four people. They were workers at a Syrian military factory. So it played as a rebel attack against the regime.

There's another way to look at it.

All fifty-four dead were civilians. Eleven were women. And who sets off car bombs in Syria? Islamic extremists, some linked to al-Qaida. They fight on the side of the rebels, and if the rebels take over, they will play a role.

Then there's the question of what role the U.S. should play.

Many Americans still think, despite two inconclusive wars over the past two decades, that the U.S. military has within its power to reorder the world, eliminate the bad guys, install U.S.-friendly regimes and watch as peace and quiet reign. All that's standing in the way is cowardly policy.

History shows that since the middle of the last century, such exercise of U.S. military power hasn't worked. It certainly hasn't worked in this part of the world.

Mideast nations have mixed feelings about the U.S. On the one hand, they assume the U.S. can fix everything if it just puts its mind to it. That should sound ironically familiar.

On the other hand, nations here believe that the U.S. has misguidedly sided with Israel, throwing away all its potential for positive influence.

And then the U.S. leads an invasion of an Arab country, Iraq, with the intention of overthrowing a hated despot, and after it succeeds, it hangs around as an occupying power, making all the mistakes it could possibly make on the way toward leaving a shattered, divided and violent country behind when it pulls out.

In fact, if the U.S. wants to end the Syrian civil war, it's not too much of an exaggeration to say that all it needs to do is come down full force on one side or the other. The civil war would end overnight as every Syrian took up arms to defend against the imperialist aggressors. There is nothing that would unite the country more than that, except, maybe, if Israel did it.

That would be the result of a cruise missile attack or any other overt U.S. military intervention. It's the opposite of Pax Americana.

The same is true of every other Arab Spring–like uprising in the region. "Leading from the rear" is the only sensible U.S. option. Any attempt to lead from the front is doomed to backfire.

What can the West do in Syria, then? Perhaps it can help the civilians who are suffering as a result of the civil war. When a new government emerges, if one does, perhaps the West can very carefully encourage it to ease up on its population, possibly with financial and material assistance.

Very carefully – because any perception that a new regime is too close to the U.S. or the West opens it to a charge of being a "puppet of the imperialists," and that strengthens the Islamic extremists.

Otherwise, all the West can do is watch carefully, be prepared to act if the civil war spills across borders, sophisticated weapons get loose or Islamic extremists try to export their revolution.

But no military assistance or active intervention. Not to the rebels.

Not to Damascus.

Chapter 17: What they know

It's natural for people to perceive today what they perceived yesterday. It's why they tend to make the same mistakes over and over.

Military strategists blame faulty planning on generals "fighting the last war." It's what they know.

Western diplomats push for more Israeli-Palestinian negotiations despite repeated failures. It's what they know.

Observers see a few hundred protesters in Cairo's huge Tahrir Square and talk animatedly about the Third Revolution. It's what they know.

If life were that predictable, it would be mighty boring. Luckily for us analysts, it isn't.

Tahrir Square was jammed in late June 2013, when hundreds of thousands turned out into the streets to call for the overthrow of Muslim Brotherhood President Mohammed Morsi.

Tahrir Square during live TV broadcast in June 2013

That was the second successful popular revolution in as many years, leading the military to depose President Morsi. A return to military rule is not exactly what the liberals had in mind.

So a few weeks later they marked one of those strange anniversaries that Egyptian revolutionaries note, a battle against security forces in which several dozen people were killed. It's almost as if they were hoping for another battle, more dead, and another date to commemorate.

Except this time, they called a demonstration, and almost no one came. A few hundred protesters wouldn't even show up in that TV picture. Which didn't prevent the breathless reports about the re-emergence of Egypt's liberals, the birth of the new campaign for freedom and democracy, the looming mass confrontation with the military rulers.

But it's not happening.

Egypt lived through two revolutions in two years. The first one threw out a hated dictator, Hosni Mubarak. The second one toppled Morsi, an ineffective, abrasive and often offensive elected president.

Both times the military took control. After the anti-Mubarak revolution, the liberals hailed the soldiers as partners. "The people and the military, hand in hand," they chanted again and again.

The euphoria didn't last long. The liberals kept marching up and down the square, demanding more freedoms, more concessions, more retribution against their enemies, and the military stepped in to restore order. Violence erupted. People were killed.

The commemoration that fizzled was for one of those deadly confrontations, a perfect avenue to channel protest against the latest edition of military rule in Egypt.

So why did only a handful of people come out to demonstrate?

It's because Egyptians are tired of all the turmoil. It has cost them too much, and they haven't seen benefits.

The young, dynamic military commander, General Abdel Fattah al-Sisi, is a popular figure in Egypt. It's no surprise that he won the election for president in a landslide, though getting 97 percent of the vote smacks more of a totalitarian-style election. No matter, Egyptians as a whole don't mind.

The majority of Egypt's people have no problem with the military running the country. They do not pine for democracy or talk about the good old days when there was an effective elected government and proper representation for all the voters.

Egypt has never had that, so there's nothing to reminisce about, get all teary-eyed nostalgic about.

Quite the opposite. Since 1952 when a cabal of officers, including Gamal Abdel Nasser, deposed King Farouk, the military has run the country, either from the front of the stage or behind the scenes. The people are used to that. There are military bases inside cities. Soldiers are as common a sight on Egypt's streets as on Israel's, though obviously for different reasons.

While Egypt was no paradise under Mubarak, at least it was quiet. That's what the people remember. Quiet enough to draw foreign investors, quiet enough to be a magnet for tourists from all over the world.

Spending a post-second-revolution summer day in Alexandria, one of the world's most beautiful and interesting cities, I saw exactly one tourist – me. A taxi driver was so out of practice that he couldn't find the famous Alexandria Museum.

Alexandria's city museum

More than once as I walked down the street, people smiled and said "Welcome," without trying to sell me anything, just glad to see a foreigner.

The Mubarak-era oppression, political arrests, corruption and inefficiency are a distant memory now to people who have experienced more than two years of turmoil and economic ruin. They long for the "good old days" of government-enforced peace and quiet, not a democracy they never had.

This is nothing new. I encountered such grumbling already in late 2011 from beleaguered businessmen in deserted downtown Cairo, just months after Mubarak was unseated.

Now add the fact that the only type of rule that could enact the sweeping economic reforms Egypt needs is military rule. Such reforms, including cancellation of subsidies on basic products and fuel, would lead to large-scale displacements and even some starvation before the ship righted itself. There would be riots of all kinds. The military would have to put them down ruthlessly. There is no other way, and that would be just the beginning.

No elected government, given the history of two revolutions in two years, would dare to even try to start the process.

Not that the current military rulers necessarily have the ability to plan and enact the reforms. They didn't even think to guard the foundation of their monument to the dead protesters in Tahrir Square the day before the scheduled commemorative demonstration, making it easy for a few vandals to wreck it and make a photogenic political statement.

The first sign that the government means business is al-Sisi's plan to slash subsidies on fuel. That's a key measure toward economic reform.

Most of the people believe the military government can restore order and bring back investments and tourists. They're probably right, at least about the restoring order part.

Even the grass-roots "Tamarod" movement, which improbably claimed more than twenty million signatures on a petition to oust Morsi and led the revolt against him, opposed protests against the military after the coup.

So is this the time for Western leaders to be pushing Egypt toward another round of elections, another round of uncertainty and turmoil, another ineffective government? Is this the time to punish the military for ruling with the support of the people? Yet that's what they have done.

The problem is that Westerners tend to see the world through the rosy prism of their own functioning democracies.

It's what they know.

Chapter 18: The second time

Sometimes, on the other hand, it's possible to learn from experience.

I used to fly home to Tel Aviv for holidays and family events. There's a direct flight four times a week. The trip takes about an hour.

Shortly after I moved to Egypt, I took the flight from Cairo for the first time. It's operated by Air Sinai, part of Egypt's national carrier, EgyptAir.

I called EgyptAir and made a reservation. They said I could pick up my ticket at any EgyptAir office and pay with my American credit card. There are several offices in Cairo, so I picked the one downtown, since I know where that is – on the same street as the main synagogue.

I took a number, waited about twenty minutes, and a friendly clerk wearing a headscarf welcomed me. I gave her my reservation number. She punched it into her terminal and – nothing.

That's where this story really starts.

The young woman got up, a puzzled frown on her face, and consulted her supervisor. A few minutes later, she came back and told me, apologetically, that I had to go to a different EgyptAir office. "It's in Shoubra," she said, writing down the address in Arabic on a scrap of paper. "It's in the Champillion building."

Air Sinai's service to Israel is not exactly EgyptAir's star attraction. No one plays up ties to Israel here. The Cairo airport website lists its flights to Tel Aviv as "inactive." That can be unnerving the first time.

I didn't know where Shoubra was, and I didn't bring my map (stupid). But it didn't really matter. There are always taxis. I stopped one and gave him the address.

Off we went, out of downtown, through a dusty business district, through a gray, rundown neighborhood, onto a wide street in another rundown neighborhood, around a traffic circle, between a row of shops with cracked fronts, and all the way, people, people everywhere, though it was midday.

After about forty-five minutes, we arrived in Shoubra, on a main street right next to the Nile. The driver pointed to a building. I paid him and got out of the taxi.

It's what we call a working-class neighborhood. Shabby, cracking apartment houses, with shops and businesses on the ground floors. I went into a pharmacy to ask directions.

A woman behind the counter smiled as I came in. I asked her where the Champillion building is. Three doors down, she said, pointing to her left. I thanked her and headed that way.

Three doors down, set back from the street in staggering formation, was a large, multistory complex with three entrances. I asked the guard at the first one where EgyptAir was. He said it's the next entrance. I asked at the next entrance. There the guard said it was in a building in the next block, back the way I came from.

I got to that building, asked the guard, and he smiled and said, yes, it's on the fourth floor. Whew. Finally.

A rickety elevator wheezed its way up to the fourth floor of the old building. I got out and looked around. There was a walkway around the dark, peeling perimeter overlooking the central space, which went all the way down to the ground floor.

There were two clothing shops, a couple other unidentifiable businesses and a hairdresser. No sign of EgyptAir or Air Sinai. I was standing outside the hairdresser's, wondering where I had gone wrong in my life, when a jaunty, round, friendly, middle-aged man stuck his head out the door and asked, with the big smile I was happily getting used to, if he could help me.

He saw me holding a piece of paper, the one I got downtown at EgyptAir, and he gently took it from me. It had a phone number on it. He whipped out his cell phone and called. After an animated minute-long conversation with gestures in several directions, he called over a skinny teenager who apparently worked there, pointed at me, gave him instructions and motioned for us to get going, again with a smile.

The kid led me back down through the elevator and out the front door, and we turned right. Even farther in the opposite direction the woman at the pharmacy first gave me. We walked and walked up the main street, probably for five minutes, but it seemed longer. Suddenly, there above me, over the ground floor of a decrepit high-rise, was a huge EgyptAir sign.

Can't miss it

I offered the boy some money, but he wouldn't take any, insisting he was going this way anyway.

It turns out that most Egyptians are so friendly and so eager to help that they will give you directions even if they don't know the way, just to be nice.

You're probably thinking this is the end of the story. Not even close. Stay with me.

I entered the large office through swinging glass doors and saw a long row of clerks. I went over to one. I told her I needed to get my tickets at Air Sinai. She said, "It's back there," motioning to her left.

I made my way past all the agents' positions, and sure enough, back behind all of them was another room. I walked in and, eureka, Air Sinai.

There were two clerks on duty. I approached one, said good afternoon, I have a reservation. Big smile, "Certainly sir, what's the number?" I gave it to him, he punched it into his terminal, and – nothing.

Let's start over, I suggested, and I gave him my travel dates. He quickly entered all the information and asked me to pay. I handed him my credit card.

A frown creased his round, friendly face. He said, "I'm sorry sir, you have to pay cash."

I made an attempt to find a working ATM nearby but failed. By then I had been out and around for nearly four hours, and I was running out of time. I stopped a taxi and rode back to my apartment to get ready for work.

The next day, I visited my usual ATM, took out the cash for the ticket, walked across the bridge to the mainland, stopped a taxi, told him "Shoubra, straight ahead," and got off where I started recognizing the place I'd been wandering around the day before. I marched proudly into the EgyptAir office, down to the end of the row, hung a left and strode into the Air Sinai office.

The same clerk was there, and he greeted me with the same smile. "You brought cash?" he asked. Indeed I did. He issued the ticket, the guy next to him took my pile of bills, and that was that. I grabbed a taxi back. The whole thing took less than an hour.

It's easier the second time.

Chapter 19: Cash for everything

Airlines are not the only places where payments have to be made in cash. It's the rule, not the exception. It's a "cash economy," with all the problematic implications for orderly commerce.

Here's how you count cash in Egypt.

You take a stack of bills, fold the whole pile in half around your index finger, then flip the bills one at a time with the thumb on that hand while counting them with the other hand.

It's quick. It's efficient. It's a necessary skill.

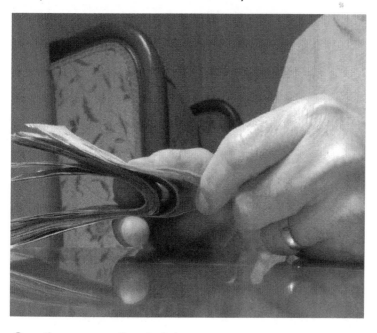

Counting money, Egypt style

In Egypt's cash economy, only about 10 percent of the people have bank accounts, much less checking accounts or credit cards.

In places like the U.S. or Israel, if you pay your plumber in cash, the assumption is he's giving you a discount because he won't give you a receipt and won't pay taxes on the job.

In Egypt, just about everybody pays cash for just about everything. So tax collection on transactions is nearly impossible.

The checkout guy at the supermarket counts just a few bills by folding them around his index finger first. It's that ingrained.

This is just one aspect of Egypt's dysfunctional economy. The economy is the most important issue facing this country. Not the Muslim Brotherhood, not women's rights, certainly not Israel. Besides the few and far between perfunctory broadsides, people don't even mention Israel. The economy will float or sink any Egyptian government. Odds favor sink.

Half of Egypt's people live near or below the international poverty line. That's an income of $2 a day per person. It's a cold, statistical way of describing the mind-numbing poverty that grips most of the people in this country.

It's only getting worse.

Half of Egypt's foreign currency reserves evaporated in the year after President Hosni Mubarak was overthrown in 2011. Subsidies drain away about a third of the budget. Unemployment is slotted at 10 percent, but that's a joke. People who work part time, even a few days a month, are considered "employed." Many workers take home less than $100 a month. Full-time bus drivers earn $50 a month.

The vast majority of Egypt's eighty-two million people are happy if they have enough cash just to provide food and shelter.

The cash economy is part of the cause and part of the effect. A cash economy means little credit. Credit drives business.

Large companies here have bank accounts and access to credit lines. Most small businesses do not. They aren't even registered with the government. Efforts to correct that with amnesties, outreach programs and assistance have failed. The tailor who fixes clothes in a little stall on the main street assumes it will do him no good to have the government looking over his shoulder, requiring him to fill out forms, and ultimately forcing him to pay taxes. Credit means little to him, except perhaps letting a favored customer pay him "in a few days" for mending a pair of pants.

Credit drives modern economies. Too much credit drives them into the ground, as with the U.S. and its sub-prime mortgages and overheated credit card debt. Too little credit stifles consumption, production and tax revenues.

It means the electricity company and the gas company send people around to knock on doors, one by one, to collect bills. They're not the only ones.

Egypt's newborn online shopping industry, if it can be called an industry, offers a payment option that sounds as if it's coming back from the last century – cash on delivery. COD. You order online, and pay cash to the guy who brings you the merchandise.

A magazine called *Business Today* offers subscriptions. It's in English, obviously aiming for foreigners and upper-crust Egyptians. There are three pay options – check, credit card or "Please collect payment."

The magazine says Egypt's total credit amounts to less than a third of its GDP. Developed economies carry about four times that level.

It's like this all over the emerging world. Badly structured economies perpetuate themselves. No credit generates no credit. Even economists don't know where to start to fix this, much less governments.

There is no easy solution. When wages are so low, credit isn't an option. When credit isn't an option, you pay cash.

And you learn how to count large piles of bills.

Chapter 20: Giving up on illegal building

It's the size and scope of Egypt's problems that can leave you gasping for breath. Take housing, for example. More than eighty million people have to live somewhere. In a cash economy, it's inevitable that construction will be off the books. In Egypt, so much housing is off the books (illegal) that the very term has been abandoned. It's called "informal," as if there's nothing to be done.

But a trip from Cairo to beautiful Alexandria brings out how damaging it is.

Pompey's Pillar is Alexandria's oldest and most famous landmark. It rises above the skyline, well back from the Mediterranean Sea. It's one of the city's few surviving remnants of Roman rule. Cleopatra's city is underwater now.

The stately pillar is both more and less than it appears.

First of all, Pompey had nothing to do with it. That Roman emperor was long gone when Diocletian built the hundred-foot-high pillar in 291 C.E. to support a statue of...himself, of course. To be fair, the engraving disclosing that little factoid was covered with rubble for centuries and the statue was gone, leading to the mistaken identification.

The pillar is guarded by two stone lions. It must have looked pretty much like this back then, if you can imagine the statue on top:

Pompey's Pillar

A short walk around the pillar brings us starkly up to date. From the other side, modern Alexandria looms just behind – ugly, block-like apartment buildings of every height, some finished, some left as skeletal blight, most of them "informal." It spoils the majesty of the site.

Modern view

How did this happen? How did a unique, ancient monument, a main attraction for tourists, come to be defaced like this?

It's a jarring introduction to modern Egypt, where everything is going wrong and has been going wrong for decades. That leaves problems on a scale so vast and so entrenched that the best that bureaucrats, and even academics, can do is try to redefine them away by calling them "informal."

Most of us live in countries that haul us into court if we so much as build a roof over a balcony without all the proper paperwork. Not here.

Likewise the unregistered economy: people working without declaring income. It's anywhere from 40 to 60 percent of Egypt's economy. No one knows exactly. It's so pervasive that there's no possibility of "cracking down" or "enforcing the law." It's just written off as the "informal economy." The loss to the state in tax revenues, and the deterioration of government services as a result, is devastating.

An Egyptian-German government-funded study that's sympathetic to the "informal settlements," as the illegal neighborhoods are known, estimates that 70 percent of Cairo's eighteen million people live in them. That's about thirteen million people just in Cairo.

And it's not just in Cairo. All along the way from Cairo to Alexandria, about 180 kilometers (110 miles), there are housing developments, towns, villages. Mosques with minarets reaching skyward. Flat, block-like schools.

It gets worse. Not only are all of them illegal – they're all built on farmland.

Illegal construction near the Nile

So are the urban sprawl neighborhoods around Cairo.

So not only is the government losing revenue, not only are people living in substandard housing with jury-rigged electricity, primitive plumbing if any, no paved roads, and the risk that the whole building might collapse at any moment – this growing and hungry nation is losing some of its best farmland to "informal" construction. Almost all of it is near the Nile or its offshoots, which provide irrigation for crops. Government attempts to build authorized neighborhoods in the desert nearby have flopped.

It's all around. The bridge that connects the Nile River island where I lived with the mainland empties on each side into veteran Cairo neighborhoods, Bulaq and Imbaba, with tens of thousands of residents. Both are made up mostly of informal construction.

All along the "Ring Road," the highway that circles Cairo, there's informal construction on both sides. There's no attempt to hide anything.

This is just one of the huge problems facing Egypt. The scope of it is overwhelming, just as poverty, pollution, health care and many other problems are gigantic beyond comprehension. No wonder the bungling Islamist government failed to fix things. Even a good government would likely be defeated by the enormity of it all.

Illegal housing next to Cairo's Ring Road

Egypt's society dates back seven thousand years. The art, construction feats and accomplishments of the ancients, preserved for our wonderment, have drawn tourists from around the world when things are quiet.

Yet when the ancient compares to the present, there is a clear esthetic and cultural drop-off. Sometimes they come clashing together in the same place, like Alexandria.

The contrast is so stark, it's as if there are two Pompey's Pillars in the same place.

Chapter 21: Cairo cough

Cairo's endemic air pollution, attributed to unregulated vehicles and smoke-spewing factories, isn't the worst of it. In late fall, everybody there seems to be coughing and sneezing, even the locals.

It's the dreaded Black Cloud.

Around that time, farmers in the Nile delta north of Cairo begin burning the waste from their rice crop. Egypt produces more than five million tons of rice a year, and along with that, four million tons of rice husks and straw. That's what they're burning.

So every year a cloud of eye-watering, throat-irritating pollution descends on Cairo for about a month.

It starts in the evening, when the cloud wafts in from the delta, trapped under the nightly thermal inversion. It's gone by morning, except for the thin layer of black dust that seems to accumulate everywhere, even in my apartment, where I almost never opened the windows because of the pollution and the pesky black flies.

The Black Cloud first appears as a wide gray line on the horizon below the reddish glow of the sunset.

The Black Cloud approaches

The yearly cloud, as with so many other things here, is part of a larger problem.

The problem has many aspects. Pollution, recycling and government failures are some of them.

In 2009, an Egyptian researcher went to the trouble of accessing NASA satellite photos to confirm that in fact, burning the rice straw was causing the Black Cloud. The research was necessary because there's almost always some kind of cloud of pollution over Cairo. It's a city of eighteen million people with two million cars, thousands of factories and precious little regulation. The air is clean only after it rains, maybe twice a year, and then only for a few hours.

In 2007 the World Bank awarded Cairo the uncoveted title of "world's worst city for pollution by particulates." That refers to all year, not just Black Cloud season.

Then there's the solid waste.

A city that size generates enormous amounts of garbage. Much of it piles up in the streets of poor neighborhoods. Some is hauled off to landfills.

Some is burned.

It used to be better than this.

When you think of recycling, you think of different colored bins where you put paper, plastic and glass. Egypt's recycling system was much more efficient when it worked.

A whole subclass of people collected garbage from door to door and took it to their neighborhood. There, they sorted through it, removing plastics, glass, metal and anything else they could sell, and fed the rest to their pigs. They ate some of the pigs, sold others and bred the rest.

They were, and still are, known as "garbagers." They are Coptic Christians. Experts say their recycling was nearly 100 percent effective.

Then came the swine flu of 2009. The Egyptian government decreed that all the pigs must be killed, and they were. By then it was clear that pigs had nothing to do with swine flu, and the "epidemic" was pretty much a bust. It was also clear that the order to kill the pigs was religious persecution against the Copts by the Muslim government. Pigs are unclean to Muslims.

That was Hosni Mubarak's government, which was openly hostile to Islamist political activity. With the Muslim Brotherhood in power, the garbagers were still there, hoping to get contracts, but getting nowhere with the government. And they didn't even dream of getting their pigs back, though they were the key to the efficient process.

So Egypt's unique system of recycling garbage was undermined by the government. Little wonder that the government is unable to promote recycling of the rice straw.

Scientists, environmentalists and experts say the potential is nearly limitless. One wrote about a little pilot plant in the Nile delta where the straw is chopped up, dried, sprayed – and it turns itself into fertilizer.

More elaborate systems can turn rice waste into medicine, plywood, cosmetics, building blocks, cattle feed, water filters, plastic and biofuel. One article said rice waste was converted into a form of cement 2,500 years ago.

All that's needed is to build the conversion facilities and provide incentive for farmers to haul their waste there. That means making it worth their while financially. That means investment of millions of dollars in factories, infrastructure, systems and research. And that's where it all falls down.

Everything seems to lead back to the economy. Egypt is facing economic collapse, reaching out for huge foreign loans that will only postpone the inevitable. It has no money for projects like converting rice husks into useable products, even if the process could prove profitable in the end.

And so the people here are sentenced to suffer air pollution the year round, and the added Black Cloud coughing spells in the fall.

Resigned to her fate, one veteran resident put it this way:

"No one comes to Cairo for their health."

Chapter 22: Uncharacteristically glum

This looks like fun.

It's the simplest Ferris wheel ever. It stands in an open-air marketplace in a poor Cairo neighborhood. It's about ten feet high, and it's run by a man who turns the wheel by hand.

For a few pennies, kids can get a little ride, holding on tight to the bar above their seat. So two children, maybe six or seven years old, a boy and a girl, sit next to each other as the man spins them slowly around.

But where's the fun? The kids look glum, the man sullen.

Ferris wheel in the market

It's like that all over the country.

One overriding characteristic of the Egyptian people is their friendliness. Simply put – they smile a lot. They banter. They joke. They're comfortable, laid-back people who chat while they sip tea, help each other, display a positive attitude.

It turns out there are limits.

It had been three years since their popular revolution overthrew longtime President Hosni Mubarak. From the optimism and energy of that heady time, it's been a steady roll downhill – economically, socially and politically.

Egypt became an angry society of protest first, ask questions later.

This was a typical week in mid-2012:

* Train engineers and conductors went on strike, suddenly stopping train service. Thousands of Egyptians jammed stations in Cairo and Alexandria, none too happy. It didn't help that the strike erupted on one of the hottest days of the year up till then, 35°C (95°F) in the shade.

* Muslims attacked Christians in a town north of Cairo. Four Christians and a Muslim were killed and a church was set on fire.

* Christians attending the funeral of the four dead at the main Coptic Christian cathedral in Cairo were assaulted by an armed mob. No one would say so officially for reasons that are hard to understand, but it's fairly clear the attackers were Muslims. Police showed up late and made the situation worse. Two more Christians were killed.

* The leader of the Copts, Pope Tawadros II, criticized President Morsi for failing to carry out his pledge to protect the Christians and their churches. After Mubarak's fall, there was a spike in attacks on the Copts, who make up about 10 percent of Egypt's population. Those who can are

leaving the country – much as West Bank Christians, most of them afraid to even talk about the persecution they face from Palestinian Muslim extremists, have been leaving by the thousands over the past two decades.

* Attempting to boost flagging tourism, Morsi's government brought in a planeload of Iranians. It kept them confined to certain historical sites, but no matter – the visit set off a riot by Salafis, Muslims of an especially extreme variety, complaining that Iranians are Shiite Muslims, and as a Sunni Muslim country, Egypt must not let them in. So the government folded, suspending the project.

What's missing was the item about quick, efficient and effective government steps to improve the situation.

There weren't any.

Many here feared that once in power, Morsi's Muslim Brotherhood would move quickly and ruthlessly to impose its strict interpretation of Islamic lifestyle on an unwilling population. Turns out that was not the main problem.

The main problem was that Morsi and his government were totally and completely incompetent. That's what led to his overthrow.

From arm-waving, angry and practically incoherent television diatribes to measures adopted and then withdrawn days later, Morsi and the Brotherhood showed that they were not up to the task of running the country.

Pope Tawadros complained publicly about the government's failure to stop sectarian clashes. The International Monetary Fund waited in vain for Morsi to implement key economic reforms to qualify for a large loan to prop up the failing economy. Strikes erupted practically every day, and stopgap measures the government took to appease the workers were just patches over old patches.

Extremist Muslims riot. Secular and liberal forces riot. Workers riot. Christians riot. Everyone fights everyone else. Police open fire. People are killed.

All the turmoil drove the sinking economy down faster and faster. It has frightened tourists and investors away. The harder it gets, the more the people riot. And that makes it even worse.

Tahrir Square, the huge downtown plaza that was the focus of both of the popular uprisings, is often a battle zone. Traffic is usually diverted away from the six-lane circle, jamming the surrounding streets, as successive groups of rioters block this street or that government building for any number of reasons, many of them justified, while protesters often maintain a permanent encampment in the middle of the square.

Just another day in Tahrir Square

So downtown Cairo, once a vibrant, joyful mix of wide streets, well-stocked stores, sidewalk vendors, cafés and night clubs, is often glumly calm.

All this is getting people down. It may be that Egypt is ungovernable, given the size and scope of its problems, but the lack of effective leadership toward any positive goal finally took its toll on the national mood.

A young Cairo woman put her finger on how it felt and what it meant.

"When people stop joking around," she said, "you know there's trouble."

Chapter 23: Too much constitution

Egyptians have approved three constitutions in three years. The last two generated complaints, demonstrations and riots, but most objections missed the point – constitutions by themselves make little difference.

The latest one, approved by 98 percent of the people who went to vote in early 2014, goes a long way toward satisfying liberal objections to the pro-Islamist constitution rammed through by President Morsi before he was deposed.

But like the others, the new one will do little to improve the critical situation Egypt faces – politically, socially and economically.

Examining the new constitution and comparing it to the Morsi version is a chore. The new one has 247 articles, even more than the 236 articles in the previous one.

By contrast, the constitution of that well-known fledgling democracy, the United States, has all of seven articles. Granted, it needed ten quick amendments to fill a glaring lack of citizens' rights , but even today, more than two centuries later, the American constitution, the bedrock of its system of government, has a brief preamble, seven articles and twenty-seven amendments, including one that was repealed.

In March 2011, a month after President Hosni Mubarak was deposed in a popular revolution, the new military rulers put forward what they called a "constitutional declaration," which was approved handily by the voters. It had sixty-three brief articles, many of them just one sentence. It guaranteed freedom of religious practice, civil rights and fair judicial and police procedures. It set up elections for president and parliament. It left the military in overall control, listing powers that included legislation, administration and security, ostensibly yielding most of these to the elected leadership but not stating that explicitly.

Those were happy times in Egypt. Mubarak, the hated dictator, was gone, and the people felt they were in charge. All around Cairo's downtown Tahrir Square, where hundreds of thousands had demonstrated weeks earlier, souvenir hawkers did a big business with revolution trinkets. There were revolutionary teacups and revolutionary tissue boxes.

Revolutionary tissues and cups

T-shirts, key chains, flags, cigarette lighters, banners, streamers, wrist bands – practically anything that could hold a logo – became a revolutionary keepsake.

Souvenirs at Tahrir Square

So people joyfully went out to vote for the constitutional declaration, calling it their first-ever free election.

It all went downhill from there.

Islamists swept the parliamentary elections because the liberal and secular forces that toppled Mubarak were too busy fighting the military – just weeks after they declared the army their closest allies and bosom buddies – while the Muslim Brotherhood used its in-place organization, coupled with the population's innate affinity to Islam, to take control of about half the parliament. Religiously reactionary Salafi Muslim groups that advocate returning to the Islam of the seventh century and are more extreme than the Brotherhood, won another quarter. The liberals won 9 percent of the seats.

A similar scenario played out in presidential elections, ending in the election of the Muslim Brotherhood's Morsi. His proposed constitution sparked riots and huge demonstrations – even though its main fault was its length. The constitution eventually approved by 64 percent in a relatively small turnout, had clauses like this:

Principles of Islamic Sharia law are the principal source of legislation.

That is not a source of controversy in Egypt. Morsi's added Article 219, infuriating the secular liberals:

The principles of Islamic Sharia include general evidence, foundational rules, rules of jurisprudence, and credible sources accepted in Sunni doctrines and by the larger community.

The liberals said that cleared the way for actual imposition of Sharia, something Morsi never even hinted at. The new constitution eliminates Article 219, much to the relief of the liberals.

Yet Morsi's document also had language like this, which the liberals preferred to ignore in their quest to demonize Morsi:

Article 43
Freedom of belief is an inviolable right.... The State shall guarantee the freedom to practice religious rites and to establish places of worship for the divine religions, as regulated by law.

Article 33
All citizens are equal before the law. They have equal public rights and duties without discrimination.

And this in the preamble:

Equality and equal opportunities are established for all citizens, men and women, without discrimination or nepotism or preferential treatment, in both rights and duties.

That's what happens when a constitution is too long and too detailed. Critics and supporters can cherry-pick what they want to emphasize, and in the end, it's too cumbersome, specific and contradictory to work either as a functioning framework for government or as a touchstone for the ordinary citizen.

The new one falls into the familiar trap – trying to fix the old one by adding more than it subtracts.

New articles expand the rights of women, outlaw religious discrimination, and a whole host of other high-sounding declarations:

Article 53

Citizens are equal before the law; they are equal in rights, freedoms and public duties without discrimination on the basis of religion, belief, gender, origin, race, color, language, disability, social status, political affiliation, geographic location or any other aspect.

Two full-blown constitutions have made little difference, despite such lofty language. That's no wonder. I remember doing a live radio interview with a university professor who was an expert on constitutions. He posited that liberal constitutions created liberal societies. I gave him half a dozen examples of the worst despotic dictatorships that had sparkling, progressive constitutions and asked him how he accounted for that. There was a long, long silence.

It doesn't work like that. An effective constitution, like the American one, is a statement of general principles. The legislature fills it out by passing laws, and those can be changed at will, providing the flexibility that any democracy needs to survive. That presumes a working legislature, which presumes a functioning democracy – neither of which Egypt has.

So where this all falls down is its collision with reality.

The military, which took over from Morsi through its appointed interim government, cracked down on the Muslim Brotherhood, declaring it a terrorist organization and imprisoning its leaders – including Morsi – and thousands of its followers. Human rights advocates report that in the first seven months after the military overthrew Morsi, more than 1,400 people were killed in clashes between protesters and the military – most of the casualties from the Brotherhood.

Journalists have been thrown in prison for the crime of reporting. Activists who were urging people to vote "no" on the new constitution were arrested.

Little wonder, then, that with a turnout of 38 percent, about 98 percent of the voters said "yes." Outcomes like that are seen only in totalitarian states and their "elections" – Soviet Russia, Syria and, of course, Mubarak-era Egypt.

January 25, 2014, marked the third anniversary of the start of the anti-Mubarak popular revolution. The first two anniversaries were celebrations, happy rallies of hundreds of thousands. The third anniversary was marked by competing protest marches in cities across the country – Muslim Brotherhood backers and liberals, each clashing in turn with security forces, leaving about fifty people dead.

The main feature of the day was the size of the protest marches. Each had a few thousand participants. The clashes made for great television, and the casualties were grist for the human rights machine – but by and large, the people, who know how to come out into the streets in their hundreds of thousands and even millions, sat this one out.

In fact, the largest demonstration was in Tahrir Square, where crowds chanted slogans and demonstrated in support of the military rulers.

After two years of constant revolution and precious little to show for it, Egypt's people are pleased that the military is in charge, whether we Westerners like it or not. They hope the military will be able to restore the order of Mubarak's dictatorship, calm things down – and, especially, fix the broken economy, starting with attracting tourists and investors who fled during all the turmoil and have not come back.

Here's the key part of that original constitutional declaration of March 2011, now forgotten in the rush of dramatic events that followed.

Article 56

The Supreme Council of the Armed Forces deals with the administration of the affairs of the country. To achieve this, it has directly the following authorities:

- Legislation

- Issuing public policy for the state and the public budget and ensuring its implementation

- Appointing the appointed members of the People's Assembly

- Calling the People's Assembly and the Shura Council to enter into normal session, adjourn, or hold an extraordinary session, and adjourn said session

- The right to promulgate laws or object to them

- Represent the state domestically and abroad, sign international treaties and agreements, and be considered a part of the legal system of the state

- Appoint the head of the cabinet and his/her deputies and ministers and their deputies, as well as relieve them of their duties

- Appoint civilian and military employees and political representatives, as well as dismiss them according to the law; accredit foreign political representatives

- Pardon or reduce punishment, though blanket amnesty is granted only by law

- Other authorities and responsibilities as determined by the president of the republic pursuant to laws and regulations. The Council shall have the power to delegate its head or one of its members to take on its responsibilities.

That is actually what the most Egyptians want today. So instead of going through all the upheavals of drafting and voting on two overblown constitutions – maybe they should have quit while they were ahead.

Chapter 24: Afghan carpets and carpetbaggers

In many ways, the Middle East stretches all the way to Afghanistan. The U.S.-led wars in Afghanistan and Iraq, for example, have the same trappings – and the same traps.

There's a new book about Afghanistan that explains, by way of a teenager's personal story, what the West doesn't know about that society, and why whatever it does there is doomed to failure. It provides lessons for the West in handling, or not handling, the Middle East as well.

The fort in the book, *A Fort of Nine Towers* (Farrar, Straus & Giroux, 2013), has only one tower. The other eight are no longer standing, writes the author, Qais Akbar Omar. It's a metaphor for the whole country, torn by decades of war after war.

We follow Qais and his family through violence, death, war, tragedy and nomadic travels back and forth across the country to try to stay alive. Yet the stories are warm, human and engaging, despite the suffering.

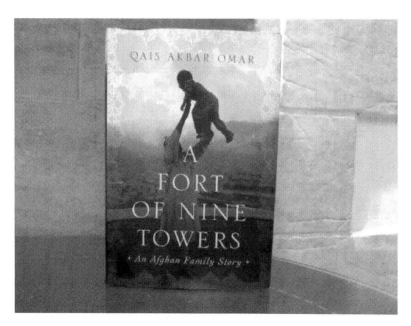

Afghanistan through the eyes of a child

The autobiographical book starts when the author, who says his first name rhymes with "rice," is eleven years old. It begins like this:

> In the time before the fighting, before the rockets, before the warlords and their false promises...before the Taliban and their madness...we lived well.

The fort is the first place they live after incessant rocket fire by competing armed factions drives them out of their home in another part of Kabul.

The writing is personal, simple, eloquent, captivating. The stories are so detailed in their fable-like content, one after the other, that it is hard to believe that they actually happened to one person. A composite is more likely. Yet the author claims that this is, in fact, the story of two decades of his life, and a veteran Afghanistan reporter confirms it's all credible.

Carpets tie the stories together.

His father and grandfather are carpet merchants, though his father is also a high school teacher and a former professional boxer. Many of the key moments in the story surround carpets, a mainstay of Afghan art, business and culture.

Thugs empty his grandfather's carpet warehouse at gunpoint, stealing all the stock. A rocket fired by militants years later sets his father's carpets on fire, destroying everything.

Qais learns the art of carpet weaving from a beautiful, magical, captivating deaf woman near the hovel where the family is forced to live during one of the wars. As a teenager, he weaves his own carpets, expands the enterprise into a neighborhood factory and supports his family.

Its travels take the family – Qais, his parents, three sisters and a baby brother he calls "the crying machine" – by car, camel, on foot and even by helicopter from place to place, looking for relatives, finding hospitable strangers, managing to stay alive.

One place of refuge is a cave.

Qais writes that the cave – and this strains credulity – is behind the head of one of the two huge statues of Buddha carved into the side of a mountain in Afghanistan. Qais describes how he can see the valley below through the mouth of the statue.

Years later, long after the family made it back to Kabul, the Taliban blew up the ancient statues, destroying them. Here is an example of the kind of writing that draws the reader emotionally into the middle of the story, the country:

> I had always expected I would see our Buddha again. But the storm of ignorance that has been raging in Afghanistan for so many decades smashed him to bits before I could return. I once lived inside his head. Now he lives in mine.

The picture the author draws of his beloved homeland is of a society riven by warring factions, divided by competing tribes and torn by pointless violence that sucks innocent people in as hapless, helpless victims.

Twice he and his father are captured and tortured by warlords but somehow survive.

Then come the Taliban. The unwashed religious fanatics terrorize the society and confine women to their homes. Qais runs afoul of them twice, thrown in prison once and later escaping a gang rape by faking a bomb scare.

Yet when the Americans start a bombing campaign in 2001, after 9/11, to defeat the Taliban and al-Qaida, the people are skeptical. They want the Taliban out, but they reject foreign occupation.

That's where the book ends. We know what happens next. After aligning with a weak, corrupt government, Western forces are targeted with deadly attacks by Afghan militants.

The same thing happened in Iraq. And the same thing happened to Israel in Lebanon.

In 1982, I went through southern Lebanon as a reporter after Israel's invasion drove out the Palestinian militants.

At the Litani River, covering Lebanon in 1982

Israeli soldiers were welcomed as heroes. But at a gas station, a man pulled me aside and warned, "We welcome you now, but don't stay too long. If we consider you as occupiers, we will drive you out." And they did. It took eighteen years, but they did.

Afghanistan is even more hostile than *A Fort of Nine Towers* depicts. The author starts out by claiming that before the turmoil, "we lived well." Perhaps they did, but history indicates otherwise.

Afghanistan has been the victim of bloody tribal conflicts for centuries. And it has been the graveyard of foreign army after foreign army.

Another recent book, *The Dark Defile* by Diana Preston (Walker and Co., 2012), relates in excruciating detail the arrogant, ill-planned and doomed 1838–1842 British invasion of Afghanistan. Tribes play the British off against each other, while the British believe they're the players. It ends in a bloodcurdling massacre.

"We learn from history that we learn no history," said my eighth-grade history teacher.

Perhaps if we read more books like these, we could spare ourselves the inevitable defeat and degradation that awaits Middle East carpetbaggers.

Chapter 25: The possible

Among the more contentious agreements of the Arab Spring era is the interim accord with Iran over its nuclear development program. Iran is not an Arab country, and its "Arab Spring" failed in 2008 when protesters charging fraud in a presidential election were brutally suppressed. The handling of the current Iran issue hints that the West may be sensing its limitations in dealing with this region.

Better late than never.

"Politics is the art of the possible," observed German statesman Otto von Bismarck in 1867.

The challenge is to figure out exactly what's possible.

Neville Chamberlain thought giving parts of Czechoslovakia to Hitler was the best possible way to stave off World War II. He was wrong.

Henry Kissinger thought a thinly disguised surrender to Le Duc Tho was the best possible way to extract the U.S. from Vietnam. He was right.

The consequences of being right or wrong about the assessments of the possible are often beyond calculation. Millions live or die.

We are now seeing an example of implementing the "art of the possible" – the agreement over Iran's nuclear program.

Powers that signed the agreement to limit Iran's nuclear development program believe it's a step toward assuring the world, including Israel, that Iran will not build nuclear weapons. Israel's government and other critics charge this is a sellout – taking the boot off Iran's neck just as sanctions were having an effect.

I won't be the first to link present-day Iran with Hitler's Germany. I've never done it before, because as the son of Holocaust survivors, I believe firmly that nothing compares to the evil of Hitler and his massacre of Europe's Jews, my grandparents among them.

Crying "Holocaust" and "Hitler" in a demagogic attempt to amplify every modern threat, like Iran, is a travesty. It offends me as a person and as a Jew. It desecrates the memory of the six million Jewish dead and cheapens the principle that the Holocaust was a uniquely horrible event in human history.

That said, there are inescapable political parallels with Iran. We can learn from them.

After World War I, the victorious West punished Germany mercilessly. It imposed economic sanctions that ruined Germany's economy. That led to a nationwide famine and runaway inflation.

My parents lived through the famine during their formative years in Cologne. As adults, they were both barely five feet tall. That's 1.5 meters. My brother and I are considerably taller. Such spurts don't usually occur twice naturally. It's not illogical to conclude that the famine stunted my parents' growth.

Frances and Ernest Lowens, my parents, in 1971

My father used to show me the one-million-mark banknote in his wallet. He told me that he would take a basketful of notes like that to the corner grocery to buy a loaf of bread – if there was any bread to buy.

After World War I, Germany was brought to its knees. And what was the result?

Hitler.

Humiliating, punishing and devastating German society created a counter-reaction that made the situation much, much worse for the world when Germans turned to an evil demagogue to rescue them.

The lesson is that sanctions are effective – up to a point. After that point, they can be disastrous.

Sanctions by themselves rarely, if ever, cause major policy changes. Sanctions did not bring down apartheid. Sanctions did not overturn Communist rule in Russia.

On a smaller scale, sanctions are not going to persuade Egypt's military rulers to let the Muslim Brotherhood back into the Egyptian political arena. Instead, they might well let Russia back in.

That's a minor example of sanctions backfiring. The Hitler case is a major example.

Of course no political parallel is perfect. Pre-Hitler Germany had a form of non-functioning democracy, while Iran is already ruled by extremists. So the practical question becomes – now that economic sanctions have decimated Iran's economy, what can further pressure accomplish?

History shows that sanctions will not bring about regime change, if that's in anyone's mind. Sanctions will not persuade Iran to scrap its nuclear development program, either.

At this point, it's clear that if Iran wants to produce nuclear weapons, it will. Not even a military strike can stop Iran. Even those who advocate attacking its nuclear facilities admit that this is not the same situation as Iraq in 1981, when a single wave of Israeli warplanes destroyed Saddam Hussein's entire nuclear program. Iran's facilities are scattered, and the key ones are well protected underground.

That leaves only the art of the possible.

Supporters of the agreement with Iran to scale back its nuclear program and limit uranium enrichment insist that it's a six-month trial period with minimal lifting of sanctions – a taste of the relief Iran can expect if it cooperates. Critics counter that Iran just has to pretend for six months while planning its next steps toward nuclear bomb building.

Backers say it gives the UN nuclear agency additional access to monitor what Iran is actually up to. Critics point out that Iran is not allowing access to the key site, where even UN experts believe weapons research is underway.

All this requires accurately predicting the future, which is impossible. That's the main problem with von Bismarck's formula. It can be tested only in the aftermath of the events it triggers. So no fast and firm conclusions can be drawn at this stage about the Iran deal. It's all "educated guesswork," an outstanding oxymoron.

The agreement with Iran is not built on trust. It's built on positive persuasion. Its drafters believe this is the best possible way to impede Iran's march toward nuclear weapons.

It they are right, it will be a landmark victory for diplomacy.

If they are wrong, Israel might find itself defending against a nuclear-powered adversary for the first time, possibly on its own, possibly with allies.

That would be an entirely new level of testing the art of the possible.

Chapter 26: Long view

"Good Lord! Look at the size of that tumor!"

Not what I was hoping to hear from my hand surgeon as she looked at the MRI of my left hand. Little did I know that in the end, it would teach a lesson about international politics.

The operation to remove the benign growth that was taking over my palm was extensive, painful and damaging. Even after several months, my poor hand was nowhere near back to normal. It will never be.

After the operation

There are two ways to deal with this.

One way is to get frustrated over the pain and the limitations. Typing, something I've been doing since I was fourteen, was a minefield of missed keys, errors and misspellings in every line. Even opening jars was a challenge. Using a screwdriver became a right-handed chore – I used to be ambidextrous. The pain was still pretty constant. So day to day, it was no fun.

The other way is the long view.

A year after the operation, most of this will be behind me. OK, so my boxing career is over, but seriously, the limitations won't be so awful. The pain will be gone. Whatever strength and feeling I have will be what there is. I am, after all, lucky to be able to use my right hand for everything that used to come naturally left-handed. My typing was never that good to begin with, and these days, I don't need hand strength to pound an old, black upright typewriter. I can correct all the mistakes without using white-out, and no one's the wiser.

I admit that taking the long view is a bit of a challenge sometimes, but it's the right way.

That applies to practically everything.

Take Syria, spying, Obamacare and Iran, for example.

President Barack Obama is taking heat for failures in all four areas. He failed to attack Syria over its use of chemical weapons. He failed to prevent spying on U.S. allies. He failed to ensure a smooth implementation of his health insurance reform. And most recently, his critics charge, he failed to hold the line against Iran's dangerous nuclear program.

A learned friend wrote recently that he supported Obama, but now he's losing patience over his "chronic inability to get in front of issues, as opposed to respond to them."

It's a widely expressed criticism, a widely felt frustration.

So let's do the "long view" test on those issues.

The problem with Syria, according to the critics, is that Obama drew a red line on the use of chemical weapons, threatened a military strike, watched

Syria cross the red line but did nothing. This obliterates the U.S. deterrent power, goes the argument.

The fact is, U.S. policy was surprisingly successful, considering that any American military move would have been counterproductive, uniting all parties in Syria against the American imperialist aggressor. Since the Iraq fiasco, hate of America has reached heights in this region that guarantee that wherever the U.S. leads, movement will be in the opposite direction.

So look what Obama accomplished. Not only did he manage to frighten the Syrians, he frightened the Russians enough to get them to force Syria to give up its chemical weapons. Wasn't that the object, unattainable through military force alone? It's said that the most effective military operation is the one that proves unnecessary. That's what this was.

So a year from now, Syria will be without all or most of its chemical weapons and without the means to produce new ones.

The scandal over the revelation that the U.S. has been spying on its allies is puzzling. It should be common knowledge by now that everyone spies on everyone. There's only one rule, violated in this case – don't get caught.

A diplomat and I often discuss sensitive matters. When we get into those areas, he moves his cell phone out of earshot. He assumes, rightly no doubt, that someone is listening, even if it's switched off. Western intelligence agencies trade clandestine information – but clearly not everything, so each country has to make up the differences for itself. It's been that way since time immemorial.

So a year from now, this artificial spying scandal will be forgotten, and perhaps the most famous spy in custody, Jonathan Pollard, will finally be free.

The rollout of Obamacare was a disaster. The health care website crashed, misdirected, mistransferred, mis-everything. There's a danger that the fiasco might deter young, healthy people from enrolling, skewing the premiums and sinking the system.

A year from now, the rocky start, while regrettable, will be forgotten. Millions of Americans who were uninsured before will be covered. If the deal is good, young people will sign up. Just as Social Security and Medicare were contentious at the beginning and are now considered bedrock of American policy, so Obamacare will become part of the landscape, and people will wonder what the fuss was about.

Iran is the trickiest of these, because it's still in flux. Critics, especially in Israel, worry that just when Iran is feeling the pinch of the sanctions, the West is going to let up without dismantling Iran's nuclear program.

The counterargument is that it's better to bring Iran into the international fold and regulate what it's doing than to isolate Iran and aim for the unattainable goal of razing all its nuclear facilities to the ground.

Also, some scholars have noted that since 1945, no one has actually used a nuclear weapon, and that lends strength to their contention that possession of nuclear weapons imposes a sensible foreign policy rather than the opposite. That applies to the U.S. and its Western allies, of course, but it's worthwhile noting that nuclear powers include un-Western and unstable Pakistan, which has also kept its nuclear weapons safely in the garage.

Of course there are limits to this long view method. It looks into the future, and nothing out there is certain.

A year from now, though I consider it unlikely, Syria could produce a full arsenal of chemical weapons from a hiding place, Western nations could retaliate against the U.S. for its spying, Obamacare could crash and burn and Iran could test its first atomic bomb.

My brother illustrated the real limits of the long view approach when I observed that if this operation on my hand is the worst thing that ever happens to me, I'll be just fine.

"Don't worry," he said. "It won't be."

Chapter 27: The rights stuff

There was a time when everyone was debating whether a U.S. attack on Syria over its chemical weapons atrocities would be good or bad for the U.S., good or bad for Israel, good or bad for the world.

Those were the wrong questions.

For decades, governments have been sliding toward a human rights–related vision of foreign policy. Inevitably, the vision is that of the West.

But the world isn't the West. Most parts of the world are not suited to Western standards. Certainly the Middle East isn't.

It's worth noting that human rights as a concept is relatively new.

The U.N. passed the Universal Declaration of Human Rights in December 1948. It's hard to argue with any of the provisions, especially if you're swinging lazily on a hammock somewhere in a Western backyard.

How could anyone question rights like these, listed in the 1948 document?

* Marriage shall be entered into only with the free and full consent of the intending spouses.

* Everyone has the right to freedom of opinion and expression; this right includes freedom to hold opinions without interference and to seek, receive and impart information and ideas through any media and regardless of frontiers.

* Education shall be directed to the full development of the human personality and to the strengthening of respect for human rights and fundamental freedoms.

The problem isn't with the rights. It's with the context. The 1948 U.N. declaration makes it the business of everyone to ensure the rights of everyone else. As a U.N. document, it implies international intervention, and by extension military action, to counter abuses of human rights.

What's the record of military action to enforce human rights?

Human rights professionals like to point to Bosnia as an example of success. One defined "success" as a situation where the human rights reality is better after an intervention than before it.

NATO intervention in Bosnia in the 1990s, indeed, stopped a cruel campaign of genocide. But the cost was high. As many as ten thousand civilians were killed in the NATO bombings. Calling that a success is a stretch at best.

And how far is this human rights-related interventionism supposed to go?

Many countries, including Egypt, abuse their women. Marriages are arranged by parents. Girls are sold to the highest bidder. Genital mutilation is commonplace. All that is in direct violation of the U.N.'s 1948 principles.

Women in Egypt's Islamic society

Logically, military intervention to enforce equality of women is not so far-fetched. It's an issue that affects tens, maybe hundreds of millions of people. If the U.S. is prepared to threaten military action after Bashar Assad's regime killed more than one thousand Syrians in a chemical attack, why not military enforcement of rights that affect many times more people?

Of course the comparison is ridiculous. It's an academic progression called *reductio ad absurdum*, taking something to its logical extreme to illustrate its shortcomings. But it makes a valid point.

Case after case is proof enough. Military action to enforce human rights doesn't work. Foreign intervention on a government level to enforce human rights doesn't work.

There is a need for a new principle to guide governmental relations in the twenty-first century: Stay out of the internal affairs of other countries, no matter how ugly. Conversely, as soon as those affairs leak across borders, take appropriate steps. Refugees must be housed. Invading armies must be repulsed. But as long as the troubles are internal – hands off.

Here are two examples:

Egypt has a military government. The Western world is busy hectoring the military rulers to bring back democracy, to call elections. As if there ever was democracy in Egypt, where the concept is poorly understood and never worked, and as if the West knows what's best for Egypt.

Egypt's economy is upside-down. Successive governments have bought internal calm through subsidizing basic products. The mushrooming subsidies have ruined the structure of the budget and threaten to bankrupt the nation. Subsidies reinforce low wages and perpetuate poverty, Egypt's most serious problem.

Eliminating the subsidies and restructuring the economy would inevitably set off riots and demonstrations during a period of transition that would be painful to millions. No democratically elected government could possibly undertake such a task in a country where popular mass revolutions have toppled two governments in two years. Only a strong military regime has the power to do what needs to be done. And indeed, President al-Sisi has put forward a plan to significantly cut subsidies to fuel, setting off some protests that were quickly put down.

Wouldn't it make more sense for the West to encourage the Egyptian military to tackle the economy instead of complaining about losing a democracy that was never there in the first place, even though the resulting violence and countermeasures would temporarily run counter to some of those cherished human rights?

The second example is Syria. Given the above, what would a U.S. attack on Syria accomplish? The opposite of what it intended. Civilians would inevitably be killed and horrific pictures would flood the world's media. Such a strike would unite Syrians and the Arab world against the American aggressors, who were encouraged to attack, no doubt, by those sneaky, evil Zionists. Lose-lose.

The role of human rights in the twenty-first century must be people to people, not government to government. Human rights groups releasing statements calling on governments to halt their abuses are pathetic. Quieter, grass-roots projects to educate people to improve their own lives are to be welcomed. Several activist groups are making progress against female genital mutilation in Africa, for example, working village by village.

That's the only way to be effective. That's the rights stuff.

Chapter 28: Proportionality? For whom?

"Look, when militants in Gaza fire rockets at Israel, then Israel has a right to respond, but with some proportionality," wrote a well-known columnist as Israel fought Hamas in Gaza. The problem was what was perceived as the high death toll in Gaza, especially compared to Israel's.

So let's do a historical exercise:

It's Dec. 7, 1941. Out of a clear, blue sky, waves of Japanese warplanes suddenly sweep over the U.S. naval base in Pearl Harbor, Hawaii. In a swift, precise strike, the attacking Japanese kill 2,403 Americans.

- In response, American political and military strategists pore over intelligence of the Japanese military formation. After consulting the Proportionality Committee (PC), they find a Japanese naval base with 2,403 soldiers. A wave of American warplanes is sent out to obliterate the base.

It's Sept. 11, 2001. Al-Qaida terrorists hijack four planes. Two of them crash into the World Trade Center in New York. Another hits the Pentagon in Washington. Brave passengers bring down the fourth. Altogether, 2,977 people are killed.

- Concluding—wrongly, it turns out—that Iraq was involved in the 9/11 attacks, and declaring—also wrongly—that Iraq was threatening the U.S. with weapons of mass destruction, the U.S. sends troops into Iraq, but not before the PC determines that its military operation must kill no more than 2,977 people there.

It's 2014. U.S. forces are fighting violent Islamic extremists in Afghanistan and along the border with Pakistan. From far away, a military pilot remotely guides a drone toward a target where high-level militants are known to be meeting. He sees that the target is a house with civilians.

- The PC delays the drone strike, fearing that civilians might be killed. It orders the U.S. military to first drop leaflets on the village warning that an airstrike is about to happen, then call everyone's cell phone with another warning, and finally shoot a firecracker at the house before carrying out the deadly drone strike. The military cancels the attack.

None of these three scenarios played out that way, though the third could still happen, as opposition to drone strikes increases.

What actually took place is that after the Japanese attack on Pearl Harbor, the U.S. joined World War II, firebombed Tokyo, killing about 100,000 people, and then brought the war to an end by dropping atomic bombs on Hiroshima and Nagasaki, incinerating 225,000 more, most of them civilians.

The U.S. invasion of Iraq resulted in a war that has taken the lives of about 200,000 people, most of them civilians, and it's still going on.

There's no PC, of course, except when it comes to Israel's repeated clashes with Hamas in Gaza. Then, suddenly, "proportionality" rings out, because of the disparate casualty figures on the two sides.

To examine what's behind this, do an Internet search for "proportionality (minus) Israel." With the exception of one article about the above Afghanistan scenario where the concept is mentioned in passing, the hundreds of articles are theoretical and legal. In practice, the term seems to apply only to Israel.

Then look at the legal articles. You'll discover that the concept of proportionality has nothing to do with numbers. It has to do with whether a conflict is justified, and whether the measures taken during the conflict are suitable in relation to the original threat or attack.

In defense of President Harry S Truman's decision to drop atomic bombs on Japan – the whole concept of human rights, out of which grows the idea of proportionality, is post–World War II. It dates to the Geneva

Conventions of 1949 and the Universal Declaration of Human Rights a year earlier.

So the proportionality concept was definitely in play in 2001, when the U.S. hit Iraq and Afghanistan to try to weed out the terrorists who attacked on 9/11. There have been many bitter complaints about those wars, but proportionality isn't one of them.

During the conflict, Hamas fired more than 3,000 rockets at Israel. Israel launched more than 3,000 airstrikes at Hamas targets in Gaza and sent troops in to destroy tunnels Hamas dug under the border to send attackers into Israel.

More than 2,000 Palestinians were killed, most of them civilians, according to the Palestinian Health Ministry. Israel claims that most of the dead were Hamas fighters. Several dozen Israelis were killed, most of them soldiers fighting inside Gaza.

Israel's honeycomb of bomb shelters, reinforced rooms in houses and especially its Iron Dome rocket defense system kept its casualties to a minimum. Gaza has none of that.

Iron Dome battery

So critics of Israel scream "proportionality." It's as if Israel needs to apologize for spending hundreds of millions of dollars to protect its citizens, while Hamas spends its money to smuggle in rockets and dig tunnels under the border, and then instructs its civilian citizens to protect its rocket launching sites by staying put in defiance of Israeli warnings to leave.

So that part of the PC appeared to be in place in Israel, which dropped leaflets from the air, group-dialed cell phones and "knocked on the roofs" of targeted buildings with low-power mortar shells before an airstrike. There is no record of any other military force in the world taking those measures during a conflict.

Yet the numbers are the numbers, and the wails of "proportionality" echo around the world like these air raid sirens outside my window http://cl.ly/3I300T3H1w22 .

Legally, Israel's operation in Gaza obviously meets the definition of "proportionality" as a fitting response to the mass rocket attacks, but the misuse of proportionality as a way to bash Israel could have a terrible result.

In past such conflicts, world bodies have ignored logic and legal definitions, ignored Israel's unique efforts to limit civilian casualties in Gaza, ignored Israel's acceptance of cease-fire initiatives even when they give Hamas a prize for its rocket salvos. Instead, Israel is lashed with official reports charging it with war crimes, crimes against humanity and intentionally targeting civilians.

The day may come when Israel throws up its hands in despair and dismay and decides that its warning measures that endanger its soldiers, which they do, are not worth it, because Israel gets no credit for them.

Though it would be most un-Israeli behavior, despite the outlandish charges — on that day of exasperation, the Israeli military might plow through Gaza with no regard for civilian casualties, killing tens of thousands—just as Truman did in Japan, just as the U.S. did for the most part in Iraq.

It could happen if world bodies, journalists and columnists continue to parrot the "proportionality" mantra without thinking about what they're writing.

Chapter 29: Contrasting tales

Here are two sets of encounters that reflect on Egypt's character. They might be related. Or not.

While he was president, it emerged that Mohammed Morsi had once come out with the old description of Jews as "sons of apes and pigs." He got a lot of nasty press for it. He deserved it. Clearly Morsi's Muslim Brotherhood is anti-Semitic – religiously, ethnically and politically.

The "apes and pigs" formula appears in the Quran as part of a lesson. The issue among theologians is whether it is literal or metaphoric. Political Islamists prefer to take it literally. It makes for a good campaign slogan. More serious experts see it as symbolic, much as Jewish commentators through the ages have noted that "an eye for an eye" in the Bible is not to be taken literally.

The point is, the Islamic formulation about apes and pigs is not a curse made up on the spur of the moment. It is an Islamic description that goes back more than a thousand years. That's why it keeps popping up.

It's a natural and ugly part of the basic ideology of the Brotherhood – "*dar al-Islam*," an Islamic Mideast, where other religions are tolerated as protected minorities at best, and there is no room for a Jewish state. That's what they believe the Quran teaches. That is their goal.

Morsi's remarks were made in 2010. That was before the revolution that overthrew longtime President Hosni Mubarak. In 2010 the Muslim Brotherhood was illegal in Egypt, and thousands of its members were in prison. Its leaders said whatever they wanted and few paid attention.

In case you missed it, here's a part of his remarks back then, referring to the futility of negotiating with Israel: "Either [you accept] the Zionists and everything they want, or else it is war. This is what these occupiers of the land of Palestine know – these blood-suckers, who attack the Palestinians, these warmongers, the descendants of apes and pigs."

Morsi tried to explain that this was about Israel, not Jews. It doesn't make much difference. But that was in 2010.

Much more troubling are the more recent pronouncements of Brotherhood figures, after one of their own became the president of Egypt.

The spiritual leader of the Muslim Brotherhood, Mohammed Badie, repeated the "apes and pigs" mantra. Esam el-Erian, another Brotherhood leader, called on Israeli Jews of Egyptian origin to come "home" for their own good: "I want our Jews to return to our country, so they can make room for the Palestinians to return, and Jews return to their homeland," he said. "Why stay in a racist entity, an occupation, and be tainted with war crimes that will be punished?"

Perhaps unintentionally, el-Erian also admitted what Egyptian officials have been avoiding for decades: Those Jews he's inviting back were expelled from Egypt en masse in 1956 after Israel's ill-conceived invasion of Sinai at the behest of Britain and France. That little fact is glossed over here, as if Jews left voluntarily because it was easier to make a living elsewhere and other such rubbish.

You would think, then, that after these Islamic racists were freely elected to run this country, the streets would be running with anti-Israel poison and anti-Semitic sewage.

Certainly it's there to some extent under the surface, and in some cases, not too far under the surface. Even so, the actual record of the Morsi government was radically different.

Its two main contacts with Israel turned out reasonably well.

First was the aftermath of the bloody raid by Islamist terrorists in Sinai in August 2012. They slaughtered sixteen Egyptian soldiers on the Israeli border, stole two vehicles and crashed into Israel, where they were killed by Israeli forces before they could carry out an attack.

Egypt and Israel quietly agreed on an increase in Egyptian forces in the Sinai to combat the Islamist militants, since that was clearly in the interest of both countries. No big fanfare, no demonstrations, no protests in Egypt. For public consumption, though, the Brotherhood blamed Israel for the whole thing.

And in November 2012, Morsi negotiated a truce between Israel and Hamas to end an eight-day Israeli air offensive in Gaza aimed at stopping incessant Palestinian rocket attacks.

There's a feeling that in the Arab world, saying something is almost the same as doing something. It's the opposite of the Yiddish "*abi gazuk*" or the Hebrew "*az amarta*," as in, "So you said it, so what?" The Arab version allows people to espouse extreme ideologies, and then go on with their lives.

I'm not excusing or downplaying the poison and the danger in the Muslim Brotherhood ideology, but I'm wondering how important it is in daily life, where it's hard to picture such hatred in these pleasant, easygoing people.

The second encounter is more of a story.

I finally got into my first argument with an Egyptian.

There's a street that runs under a bridge eastward from the Nile in a poor Cairo neighborhood called Bulaq. Along and in this street, for more than a mile, merchants set up racks of clothes of all shapes, sizes and colors.

Fashion avenue

Lining both sides of the street are shops, many also selling clothes, but others offering other merchandise. It's where I got my fresh peanuts in the shell, for example.

Another shop sells cheap watches.

It's a tiny, one-man operation. The old, peeling shop is about six feet wide and ten feet deep. I bought a handful of watches for presents. The shop owner, Hassan, a man about my age, slowly added up the bill aloud in Arabic, noting that I'm obviously a foreigner. It came to fifty-five pounds. I gave him seventy. He gave me five back and started putting the watches in little bags.

Hassan and his little shop

I weighed what to do. He owed me ten pounds. That's about a buck and a half. But it's a business. So I pointed out gently that I'd given him seventy. Ah, he said, throwing up his hands in a gesture of apology, and got out fifteen to give me as change. No, I said, taking the ten and returning the five, you already gave me five.

He kept trying to give it to me and I kept saying, "No, we're good."

By then a poor, elderly man in a shabby, floor-length gray galabiya, a dirty turban and a scruffy white beard had walked in and sat down on the only chair. There's room in there for the owner, one customer and one other person sitting on the chair.

At an impasse with his obstinate customer, me, Hassan suddenly smiled broadly. You could almost see the comic-book light bulb over his head. He handed the five pounds to the old man, who said "thank you" profusely, as one can do in Arabic. Except he was thanking me, not the man who gave him the money.

So there are the two encounters. They might be related. Or not.

Chapter 30: It's over for the Jews

The demise of Cairo's fabled Jewish community came despite its public identification with the Morsi regime and its purposeful distancing from Israel. It was just a matter of time.

Two elderly ladies dressed in black, one behind large, dark sunglasses, sat quietly in the front row of chairs set up in the courtyard of Cairo's downtown synagogue.

The coffin of Carmen Weinstein, their leader for the last nine years, the force behind the tiny Jewish community of Cairo, had just been carried past them on its way to burial at the cemetery she had worked so hard to preserve.

Carrying Carmen Weinstein's coffin

The two old ladies, part of the community and symbols of its demise, appeared to realize what this meant. They spoke to no one, not even to each other. What could they say?

Their new leader had the courage to express what most people do not want to think about – more than two thousand years of continuous Jewish life in Egypt is coming to an end. Magda Haroun herself is "only" sixty, one of the youngest of the forty or so remaining Jews of Egypt. No Egyptian Jewish men attended the funeral. There may not be any left in Cairo. Likewise, no children.

Where Carmen Weinstein's quest was to preserve Jewish life in Egypt dating back to the Bible, Magda Haroun stated a different goal.

Magda Haroun

"I promise to take care of you until God receives us," she told the two old ladies and the rest of the two hundred people, almost all of them non-

Jewish guests, seated in the courtyard, as she starkly acknowledged the dim future of this "unfortunately dying community."

The battle is over what will be left behind.

Carmen Weinstein, who died in her Cairo home at age eighty-two on April 13, 2013, was a fighter. She fought Egyptian governments to restore ancient synagogues and won. She fought for restoration of the ninth-century Bassatine Cemetery south of downtown and won that fight, too, until Egypt defeated her. Now the cemetery is overrun by seeping sewage, garbage and squatters.

Her mother is buried there, but years ago she stopped trying to take care of the grave. Rabbi Andrew Baker of the American Jewish Committee, who went around the city from site to site with her for twenty years, visited the grave at the deteriorating cemetery with Mrs. Weinstein a month before she died. "I don't come here anymore," she told him.

Egypt overwhelmed her and her community and her cemetery. Most recently the population explosion, collapse of the economy and absence of effective government undermined her quest to preserve the place where Jews have been buried for 1,300 years.

But not even the cruelest of Egypt's often ruthless rulers over the last twenty centuries managed to defeat the Jews of Egypt the way that one modern leader did.

Gamal Abdel Nasser drove Egypt's Jews into exile in the 1950s. Part of the context was the creation of the State of Israel and Egypt's wars – its humiliating defeat at the hands of the new and poor Jewish state in 1949 and Israel's participation in the ill-conceived French and British attack aimed at restoring the Suez Canal to foreign control in 1956.

In a whirl of nationalist xenophobia, Nasser responded by expelling foreigners from Egypt. British, French, others – and 65,000 Jews. The difference was – the Jews were Egyptians. They were there before Islam was born, long before modern Egypt was created.

Today there are Egyptians who mark the start of the slow but steady deterioration of their nation with Nasser's expulsion of the Jews. For twenty centuries, leaders of all persuasions had incorporated Jews into their governments and economies, and they benefited. Nasser threw them out, and the cosmopolitan, quasi-European cultural element of a crucial part of Egyptian society exited with them.

Author Lucette Lagnado describes pre-Nasser Cairo in an autobiographical book that centers on her father, *The Man in the White Sharkskin Suit* (HarperCollins, 2007). She writes of a vibrant downtown, with glittering cafés and upscale hotels catering to the literati, both Egyptian and foreign.

Some of the places she mentions still survive today, like Groppi's café, but without the glitz, without the class.

Groppi's café is still there

The Europeans are gone. The Jews are gone.

A few hundred, perhaps a few thousand, managed to stay behind despite Nasser, but not enough to form a critical mass. The yeshiva named for its teacher, the great twelfth-century Jewish scholar Moses Maimonides, the Rambam, deteriorated into a roofless ruin. The Ben Ezra synagogue, home of the unique Geniza repository, with its documents describing Jewish life in Egypt for more than a thousand years, suffered from neglect.

And the cemetery, already in use for three hundred years when Maimonides moved to Cairo from his native Spain, began to disappear under the weight of slums, thieves and unregulated urban sprawl.

Carmen Weinstein set out on a rearguard, last-ditch campaign to preserve Jewish heritage in Egypt. Though she never admitted it, the abrasive, aggressive yet cultured leader must have known that her quest was only to guard the physical remnants of a Jewish life that was slowly disappearing.

She had the synagogues and cemetery restored. She battled organizations of Egyptian Jews in the U.S. and France who wanted to "rescue" the sacred books and ornaments of the Egyptian Jewish community by taking them out of there. She adamantly refused.

Magda Haroun promised to carry on that battle, while admitting that it's a fight over things, not over life itself.

"I pledge to take care of Jewish heritage and turn it over to the Egyptian people," she said, with Carmen Weinstein's coffin lying in the synagogue behind her. "It is their heritage. They need to remember that Jewish people were involved in all aspects of Egyptian life."

The message was clear to the two old ladies in the front row. It was clear to everyone.

It's over.

Chapter 31: Spotted in Alexandria

As in Cairo, there are few Jews left in Alexandria, known as Egypt's second city, set beautifully along a curving Mediterranean coastline. A visit to Alexandria's main synagogue brought home starkly how Jews no longer play an important role in Egypt.

I chuckled when I saw the Hebrew sign hanging prominently in the Eliahu HaNavi synagogue: "Do not chatter during the prayer service or the reading of the Torah."

It's exactly like the signs in synagogues all over Israel. In fact, it probably came from there.

Inside the synagogue

It means that gossiping during prayer services is a problem in synagogues around the world. I know that. I can speak for incessant chattering in synagogues in the U.S., Israel and several cities in Europe. And now Egypt.

But there aren't enough Jews left in Alexandria to make much of a ruckus.

I was all alone in the cavernous, ornate synagogue that once seated a thousand worshippers, admiring the marble columns and the white, carpeted stone stairs that lead up to the Holy Ark, taking a picture of that sign, when I heard someone walk in.

"*Asalaam aleikum*, Mark Lavie!" said a man behind me.

I sucked in my breath involuntarily, and my blood froze. Now the Egyptian *muhabarrat*, secret service, is coming after me? Now, after I've been here off and on for four years and I'm almost done?

I turned slowly.

Sitting in the front row of seats was a dapper little man. Dark skin, black and white moustache, beige jacket, tie, snap-brim cap. I looked at him suspiciously. He just smiled. He's apparently pulled this little trick before.

"I saw your passport," he chuckled. "That's how I know your name."

Well, of course he did. Color returned to my cheeks, and I started breathing again. He said his name was Abed el-Nabi.

Abed el-Nabi, comedian

The synagogue was first on my list of places to see in Alexandria. I had spent most of my time in Cairo through the years, and my day off was a chance to fix that. I boarded a train at 8 a.m., arrived in Alexandria at 10:30, took a taxi to the seacoast, and had a cup of Turkish coffee at a sidewalk café while admiring the Mediterranean and the view of the city.

Alexandria's Mediterranean beach

Then I started walking in the direction of the synagogue.

Suddenly, there it was, set back from a downtown shopping street behind a high fence of iron bars. I was told that there wasn't much chance for me to get inside, so I stuck my camera through the fence and took a picture.

Alexandria's Eliahu HaNavi synagogue

That brought a young, gruff guard out of a little wooden hut inside. He approached me from the other side of the fence. I explained to him that I wanted to see the synagogue. He told me to go around to the side entrance.

It's a big compound, and the side entrance is back down the main street and up a narrow side street. I found it and waited. Nothing happened. I called a phone number in my guidebook, but it was not in service.

Well, this isn't working, I thought. So I went back to the main gate. A second young Egyptian guard joined the first one. He asked for my passport. I gave it to him. It was my American passport, of course. My Israeli one was safely tucked away in a hiding place back in my apartment.

The guard took my American passport and told me to go back around to the side gate.

There, a third guard was waiting with my passport, which he was examining. Satisfied, he unlocked the gate, motioned for me to come in, and took my passport into the guard station, which has an engraved sign over it that says "Jewish Community, Grand Rabbinate." Not anymore.

I walked through the spacious courtyard, paved with stone and lined with trees and plants, and climbed the wide, majestic steps to the synagogue.

A woman with an Islamic headscarf greeted me at the door and unlocked it for me, telling me that the building is open from 9 a.m. to 2 p.m. but there aren't any services there anymore. Not enough Jews, she said, taking care to explain that Jews need ten men to pray in public.

She left me alone inside, and I walked to the front. That's where Abed el-Nabi had his fun with me. He didn't know I'm an Israeli and I might be touchy about being "spotted."

He's one of a handful of Jews left in Alexandria. He's been the caretaker of this synagogue for twenty-seven years, he said. He's sixty-three.

We communicated in a fun mixture of English, Hebrew and Arabic. He told me that when he started working here, there were still two thousand Jews in Alexandria, which was probably an exaggeration.

Once, though, there were at least forty thousand. Jews were a key part of the fabric here from the time Alexander the Great founded the city in the fourth century B.C.E. Once there were seventeen synagogues in the city, but now there's only this one. "No Jews," Abed said with a shrug.

So there are no regular religious services in the city, just as in Cairo. But there's a subtle difference between the two.

In Cairo, for the High Holy Days and Passover, the Jewish community brings in a rabbi from France. Services are attended by diplomats, foreign Jews working in the city and the few remaining Jews of Cairo.

Abed said for those holidays, Alexandria brings in a rabbi and a congregation from Israel.

There's a slight undercurrent of distancing from Israel that one can feel in the Cairo Jewish community – what's left of it. Egyptian Jews are proud that their community predates Israel, was there for many centuries before the state was founded, and stands on its own – or did, before President Gamal Abdel Nasser expelled most of the Jews and foreigners from Egypt in the 1950s. The heads of Cairo's Jewish community subtly keep Israel at arm's length.

But they don't exactly identify with Israel in Alexandria, either.

Abed el-Nabi told me a bit about the synagogue, noting proudly that "it's the largest synagogue in the Middle East."

Well, except for Israel, I said.

"Israel? Israel is part of Europe," he laughed. "It's not the Middle East."

Chapter 32: Not exactly kosher

The disappearance of a Jewish presence in Egypt produces challenges for an Orthodox Jew living and working in Cairo. A major one is keeping the Jewish dietary laws, eating "kosher." You do the best you can.

There's one synagogue that's still active, but "active" is a bit of an exaggeration. The Sha'ar Hashamayim (Heaven's Gate) synagogue is downtown – a big, jarring, you-can't-miss-it art deco structure set back a few feet from the traffic.

Cairo's downtown synagogue

I went there on Saturday, the Jewish Sabbath. I walked twenty minutes from the hotel where I was staying then, clipping my door key to my belt, carrying my prayer shawl and prayer book (along with my passport) in a bag, wrapping the cloth handles around my arm as a sort of garment. There is no *eiruv* ritual boundary marker in Cairo, so according to Jewish religious law, I'm not allowed to carry anything, and that's the best I could do.

Guards relieved me of my passport at the gate outside. Two Egyptians, a man and a woman, greeted me at the entrance and asked me to sign the guest book. I said, politely, that I couldn't. They didn't understand why not. I explained to them that I wasn't allowed to write on the Sabbath. They had never heard of such a thing. Eventually the man picked up the book and asked me my name and where I was from. I told him, and he wrote the information down. Crisis averted.

Once inside, I saw the typical Sephardic layout of the synagogue, with the platform for reading the Torah toward the back, a few rows of shiny wooden pews in front of and behind the platform, then pews on each side facing the center. The ornate, carved Holy Ark stood in front, up a few steps. There was an old Sephardic Torah scroll perched on the reading desk, not in the Ark.

I wasn't expecting an actual service. I know there are not many Jews left in Cairo. But I wasn't expecting to be alone, either. We were, how shall I put it, nine short of a *minyan*, the ten people needed for public prayer.

There used to be active, vibrant Jewish communities in Cairo and Alexandria. After the expulsions of the late 1940s and mid-1950s, perhaps a few dozen Jews remain, most of them in their eighties. They were lying low then, and all the more so later, with the Muslim Brotherhood in power. Their trademark center-city synagogue is mostly a museum.

Arguably the most famous synagogue here is Ben Ezra, where the Cairo Geniza was discovered – the treasure trove of discarded sacred texts and documents that has shed light on a thousand years of Jewish life. It's in the old Coptic Christian section, and it is a museum without other pretensions.

Ben Ezra Synagogue is a museum now

Egyptians run the site. I was there one day when a Japanese tour group arrived. One man wanted to know why the synagogue faces east. The guide hemmed and hawed. I volunteered to explain that Jews face Jerusalem when they pray, answering a few other questions, and everyone was grateful.

So in visiting two Cairo synagogues, I saw a total of one Jew. Me.

In Cairo, praying every morning – turning toward the corner of my apartment that faced Jerusalem – was a lonely experience.

Grocery shopping was a matter of stocking up on fresh fruit and vegetables from the little store downstairs, then going through the supermarket nearby, reading labels. I was surprised to find some products with a U or a K, declaring them kosher. Peanut butter, olive oil, sometimes tuna and salad dressing. No one else appeared to know what the letters mean. Meat was not a problem – I'm a vegetarian.

And there's always *koshary*.

Making koshary *in front of you*

Koshary is one of Cairo's signature fast foods. It's made of pasta, rice, lentils, chickpeas and fried onions, with a tangy tomato sauce on top. A meal-size portion costs about 75 cents. There was a *koshary* stall downstairs, next to the fruit and vegetable store. *Koshary* was all they made, so there was no serious *kashrut* problem. One guy inside the little hole in the wall cooks the components, and the young man outside puts it all together for you as you watch, spooning it into a foil container in layers. The sauce goes into a little bag, and he ties it shut. It's tasty and fast.

Its name has nothing to do with kosher. So *koshary* isn't exactly kosher. But on the larger scale of Jewish life in Cairo, it's close enough.

Chapter 33: Israel's unreporte

Many times over the years, Egypt has tried to t
peace settlement. It's in Egypt's interest, removi
one of two Arab nations at peace with Israel, erasing the stain of the 1979
Camp David Accords, when only the first part – an Egypt-Israel peace
treaty – was implemented, but the framework for an Israeli-Palestinian
accord was not.

In public, at least, Egypt has put most of the blame on Israel, though in
private, some Egyptian officials have expressed exasperation with the
pesky Palestinians over their incessant squabbling and complaining.

History, too, raises some pertinent questions.

My eighth-grade history teacher put it this way: "Everything depends on
where you start your history."

So where do we start the history of Israel and the Palestinians?

Nov. 29, 1947, when the U.N. voted to partition Palestine into a Jewish
state and an Arab state? The Jews accepted it. The Arabs rejected it, but
despite the war they declared on the Jews, with the stated object of
throwing them into the sea, the Jewish state survived while the Arab state
was never born. Jordan and Egypt swallowed up its territory. Yet Nov. 29 is
the date today's Palestinians chose to ask the same U.N. to recognize their
state. The irony is too bitter.

How about June 1967? That's when Israel occupied the West Bank, Gaza
Strip, Golan Heights and Sinai Desert. Its army crossed the cease-fire lines
drawn in 1949 at the end of the above-mentioned war. In other words, the
"border" of the West Bank, now accepted by practically everyone as a
sacred frontier drawn by God and handed down from generation to

was in fact just a cease-fire line that held for all of eighteen of the seven-thousand-year recorded history of the Middle East.

Maybe July 2000, when Israel's prime minister offered Palestinian leader Yasser Arafat a state in more than 90 percent of the West Bank, all of Gaza, parts of Jerusalem and a corridor through Israel between the West Bank and Gaza – something that has never existed, certainly not within the "holy" pre-1967 "borders." To the dismay of the host, President Bill Clinton, Arafat turned down the offer, walked out of Camp David and slammed the door. A violent uprising broke out two months later, and six thousand people died, most of them Palestinians.

Certainly Israel has done stupid things, like building settlements in lands it will one day likely evacuate, as it already has in Gaza. Israel has been guilty of acts of cruelty and has elected some bad leaders. None of those are decisive, though the world usually focuses on those aspects.

And all the above is well-known historical fact. So let's start somewhere that isn't so well known.

November 2008.

A year of negotiations between high-level teams of Palestinians and Israelis has come to an end. Israeli Prime Minister Ehud Olmert shows a map to Palestinian President Mahmoud Abbas. It delineates a Palestinian state in 93.5 percent of the West Bank, all of Gaza, ceding Israeli land to make up the 6.5 percent – including that corridor between the two territories – also the Arab neighborhoods of Jerusalem, and shared control of the holy sites in the Old City.

Olmert said, "Sign this." Otherwise he would not give Abbas the map, knowing from bitter experience that any proposal handed to the Palestinians simply becomes the starting point of the next round of demands. This was Israel's final offer. Abbas knew that.

So Abbas emulated his predecessor, turned around, left the room and never met Olmert again. The chance was lost for good within a month, when Israel invaded Gaza to try to put a stop to incessant rocket attacks.

Olmert's offer of a Palestinian state in the equivalent of all of the West Bank, Gaza and significant parts of Jerusalem was never properly reported at the time. Olmert didn't make it public then, apparently because it did not result in an agreement, and local media did not disclose it.

The Israelis didn't have to make it public. The Palestinians did.

On March 27, 2009, the chief Palestinian negotiator, my old friend Saeb Erekat, a fellow night owl who was always ready with a comment on current events at 2 a.m., went on Al-Jazeera satellite TV and spelled it out. He said then that Abbas "could have accepted a proposal that talked about Jerusalem and almost 100 percent of the West Bank."

Then he quoted the response Abbas gave:

" 'I am not in a marketplace or a bazaar. I came to demarcate the borders of Palestine – the June 4, 1967, borders – without detracting a single inch, and without detracting a single stone from Jerusalem, or from the holy Christian and Muslim places.' This is why the Palestinian negotiators did not sign...''

Erekat "forgot" to mention the Western Wall, a key Jewish holy site in Jerusalem that Erekat insists would be part of the Palestinian state

No one else seemed to notice it at the time, even though Erekat said this in Arabic on television, and he repeated his words a few days later at a public gathering in Hebron. I spotted the translation of his Al-Jazeera interview on MEMRI and sounded the major-breaking-news alarm, but the bureau chief at The Associated Press in Jerusalem, where I worked at the time, along with the chief West Bank correspondent, determined that it was not newsworthy and banned me from writing about it.

I will not speculate about their motives. Suffice it to say that later, when the official appointed by Abbas to investigate Palestinian corruption resigned his post in disgust for lack of backing from Abbas, took fourteen boxes of incriminating documents with him and offered the story to the AP – he was turned down. When Israel's Channel 10 TV broke the story, the AP played it down, covering it only grudgingly and putting the emphasis on sexual misconduct by a Palestinian official instead of the first clear evidence of where those billions of dollars and euros of foreign aid to the Palestinians actually went.

As for me, instead of resigning over these and other journalistic debacles, which I considered, I engineered my transfer to Cairo.

The decision not to report on the 2008 peace plan was a critical mistake in judgment. Had it been made public, had leaders, diplomats and activists become aware of it, it could have changed the focus of peace efforts from knee-jerk demands and pressure on Israel to a realistic approach toward the Palestinians.

By then, you see, the Palestinians had painted themselves into a corner.

Chances are the real reason for their timidity in 2008 was the refugees. About 700,000 Palestinians fled or were forced from their homes by Jewish soldiers during that war that followed Israel's creation. They were housed in camps along Israel's borders, in the West Bank, Gaza, Jordan, Syria and Lebanon. They have been kept there by Palestinian and Arab leaders, with the willing and continuing cooperation of the U.N., to be a festering sore, bolstered by the promise that they would one day return to their homes in Israel. After four generations, Palestinians claim their numbers have reached about seven million, and all are considered refugees from Palestine. All have been promised the right to return "home."

The figure of seven million is completely ridiculous, of course. I have failed to find another population that has increased tenfold by birth in the space of sixty years. It means that several million people are fraudulently getting assistance from UNRWA, the U.N. agency set up to aid the refugees but instead works actively to perpetuate the refugee problem and reinforce blame and hatred of Israel.

This exploding population myth has made it even harder for the Palestinians to settle the conflict and live quietly in a new state.

Arafat and now Abbas said they want a state in the West Bank and Gaza. Pulling these two threads together, it means they want a Palestinian state, and they also want most of their people to go live in someone else's state. For sure there are winks and nods in the direction of some sort of other arrangement, but no Palestinian leader has ever told his people, "Sorry, you will not be going back to that village that is now under the runway of Israel's international airport; you will be fortunate to live instead in a free Palestinian state in the West Bank and Gaza." If Arafat couldn't do it, no one can.

There have been sporadic reports about this episode over the years. Some blame Abbas for turning down the 2008 proposal, some say Abbas wanted more of the West Bank and others note that Abbas showed some willingness to compromise over refugees. Quibbling over the percentages, when the total is 100 percent and the offer includes that corridor, is not serious negotiating. And on the refugees – Abbas has made similar hints in public, and then quickly retracted them when confronted by his peers. And blaming Olmert for resigning is a copout – Israel's internal politics are not his problem.

It typically takes the Palestinians at least a year to come up with an alternative form of history to explain why they passed on peace. In 2001, it was something like, "Barak wasn't polite." Really. I'm still waiting for a narrative to excuse their passing up on a state of their own for a second time seven years later.

The ignored 2008 plan is always relevant, because Israel is constantly battered for "intransigence." The facts above show otherwise.

The downward slope into insoluble stalemate, despair and violence started in July 2000 and got its last fatal push in November 2008. Between those two dates, Israel withdrew from Gaza. Palestinians, tired of the corruption and nepotism of the party headed by Abbas, voted for Hamas, and when Abbas refused to yield to the verdict of his own people, Hamas pitched his forces out of Gaza.

That was two years after Israel pulled out of Gaza. The Palestinians had a chance for independence and glory. Instead they chose rockets and war.

And so we arrive at today. Negotiations are pointless. An understanding of the background will help us all realize that the peace process reached its logical conclusion, and it did not produce peace. Twice.

An understanding of where this all comes from, and especially the sorry events of November 2008, gives an entirely new perspective to the problem.

Because everything depends on where you start your history.

Chapter 34: The U.S. Mideast obsession

Despite all the international attention and Israel's own obsession with its role in Middle East politics in general and Arab Spring in particular, the Arab world itself does not focus on Israel that much. Arab nations are much more concerned with their monumental internal problems.

Washington, on the other hand, appears to have an obsession with the tiny Israel-Arab conflict involving a number of people equal to only about half of Cairo's population, a sliver of the Middle East.

There's a way to explain it with a little joke.

"Because he can" is the second line of a somewhat raunchy two-liner about a dog's physical capabilities.

What does that have to do with the renewed efforts toward a peace agreement between Israel and the Palestinians?

At first glance, not much.

U.S. Secretary of State John Kerry has traveled to the region many times in his first months in office. At this rate he might break the record of George W. Bush's top diplomat, Condoleezza Rice. She was in Jerusalem so often that I joked about making her pay Israeli taxes.

The main difference is the circumstances. Rice was here to promote Mideast peace talks. Kerry was here to restart Israeli-Palestinian talks.

If it was not evident before, as it should have been for decades, now it's clear that negotiations between Israel and the Palestinians are not "Mideast peace talks."

The events of the past three Arab Spring years have shown that. The Mideast is not just about Israel and the Palestinians. It's not even primarily about Israel and the Palestinians.

For all those decades, Arab leaders, joined by many in the West, bought the line that if we can just solve that tiny little problem between Israel and the Palestinians, the Middle East will be on its way to peace and quiet.

Green light for peace at Jerusalem's entrance?

It actually might have been true, to some extent, as late as 1979, when Egypt and Israel signed the two-part Camp David Accords. The first part was the peace treaty. The second was a blueprint for solving the Israeli-Palestinian conflict. Neither of those sides was the least bit enthusiastic about the formula, and it died a quiet death. That left Egypt isolated in the Arab world, a peace treaty with Israel but no second chapter.

That reinforced the already strong notion that Israel was the problem. Israeli itself, or at least its occupation of the West Bank and Gaza, was a thorn in the side of the Arab world that must be removed, they said, and then everything would work itself out.

So the world — Arab and Western — started paying completely disproportionate attention to a conflict that, empirically speaking, is among the smaller crises the world faces. While several thousand Israelis and Palestinians were killed in two rounds of violence over two decades, anywhere from 300,000 to one million people died in Darfur over a similar period, but activists there struggled and failed to persuade the world to care about that cruel conflict in Sudan.

The results of the Arab Spring uprisings have made it obvious how this all fits together — or doesn't.

In Syria, more than 150,000 people have been killed in a civil war that has been marred by massacres and abuses on both sides. Several million Syrians have been driven from their homes. More than a million are refugees in neighboring countries.

Libya has descended into chaos. Yemen is teetering.

Egypt's military is back in charge after the Muslim Brotherhood government of President Morsi made all the possible mistakes and didn't even come close to improving a critical economic situation that even a good government might not be able to fix.

What does all that have to do with Israel and the Palestinians? Nothing. What does it have to do with American diplomacy? Everything.

From the beginning, the U.S. administration could seemingly do nothing right. It backed the discredited regime of Egypt's Hosni Mubarak until it was overthrown, and then forged tentative ties with Morsi's regime, sparking outcry from all sides. It followed the lead of Europe in the Libyan civil war, drawing criticism of its lack of leadership. It dithered and stalled over Syria, fending off strident calls from the interventionists to arm the rebels or even blast President Bashar Assad's strongholds with cruise missiles.

There's a reason for all that. Many Americans don't like to consider it, because they still believe that not only can American military power correct the ills of the world, but also that it is a kind of sacred American duty.

The reality is that the U.S. no longer has the political clout in this part of the world that it once had. The last of it was lost in Iraq, when President Bush sent in his army to depose a dictator, claiming falsely that he had stockpiles of weapons of mass destruction.

The U.S. fought its way through Iraq, alienating practically everyone in Iraq and infuriating the Arab world. By the time President Barack Obama pulled the last of the combat troops out, America was what my university logic professor called a "reliable anti-authority." In this case, it means whatever the Americans try to do in this region will backfire.

So the only way the U.S. can realistically involve itself in the post–Arab Spring Middle East is by what its critics disparage as "leading from the rear." That means maintaining contacts with regimes, opening lines of communication with rebels and trying to influence policy, but gently and quietly. Anything beyond that is automatically counterproductive.

Except when it comes to Israel and the Palestinians.

Kerry is welcomed by both sides. Both have reasons to accommodate U.S. desires. It took him six trips, but he got the talks restarted. A rare victory.

Of course, unless the U.S. plans to impose a solution, the talks themselves will go nowhere.

Even the consistently superficial Israeli-Arab columnist Sayed Kashua pointed out that Kerry has only managed to bring back the same negotiators who have failed again and again. The last time was in 2008, when Israel offered a Palestinian state in the equivalent of all of the West

Bank, plus Gaza and the Arab neighborhoods of Jerusalem, yet that did not produce a peace accord. Other issues scuttled the talks, as they have before – Jerusalem, refugees and the like.

It's unlikely that a similar offer will emerge from the current talks.

Never mind. It's clear that the U.S. has no hope of significantly shaping the immediate future anywhere else in this region.

So why, when there are real issues and real problems in the Mideast, does John Kerry spend so much time restarting Israeli-Palestinian talks that are practically guaranteed to fail?

Because he can.

Chapter 35: Dam shame

"We're friends, right?" asked Moussa, one of the few Egyptians who knew I'm an Israeli. Whenever he started out like that, I braced myself.

"It says here," he began, pointing to his computer screen, "that Israel is behind Ethiopia's plan to build a dam on the Nile and steal Egypt's water. Is that true?"

Ethiopia's dam was the story of that week in Egypt. The Nile is literally Egypt's lifeline. Any threat to the flow of water in the wide river endangers the country's existence.

For years Ethiopia has been thinking about building a dam to generate hydroelectric power on its part of the Nile, just as Egypt did in the 1960s when it built the Aswan High Dam in the southern part of its country. That also stopped the yearly flooding of the Nile Delta, and that made life easier.

The Nile starts in two places in northern Africa. One branch, the Blue Nile, begins in Ethiopia. The two tributaries converge in Sudan and run northward through the length of Egypt.

Other than the Nile region and the Mediterranean and Red Sea coasts, Egypt is a barren, forbidding, steaming desert. Thousands of years of Egyptian life, culture and religion have centered on the river. It is not too farfetched to say that the Nile is Egypt, and Egypt is the Nile.

Egypt's Nile lifeline

Any perceived threat to the waters of the Nile sets off near-panic in Egypt. Estimates of the proportion of Nile water originating in Ethiopia range up to 70 percent. Images of the Nile's level dropping by 70 percent, to the point that you could walk across it without getting your ankles wet, dance across the minds of Egyptians in a daytime nightmare.

It's nonsense, of course.

If all Ethiopia wants to do is generate electricity, then the water that spins the turbines goes back into the river and flows into Egypt.

If Ethiopia wants to use some of the water to develop its agriculture by irrigation, it's pretty clearly entitled to do that, despite a colonial-era agreement that appears to give Egypt the right to the current flow of water.

But none of that matters in a society as tense, emotional and jumpy as Egypt in its post-revolutionary state. And it doesn't exempt Israel from taking the blame.

I assumed Moussa was reading one of the fringe sites of craziness and conspiracy theories that abound here. He seemed genuinely worried that Israel had contrived the Ethiopia dam story as cover for the fact that it was really planning to steal the water for itself, so I asked him how, exactly, Israel was supposed to transport the stolen water over 2,500 miles of desert? He hmmmed.

I stopped myself from saying that Israel would use its top-secret satellite-armed laser beams to vaporize the water in Ethiopia and then condense it into rainfall over the Negev – because here, they'll believe anything about Israel and its extraterrestrial powers.

There's this cartoon, for example:

Political cartoon blames Israel

It's captioned, "Wanting Blue," a reference to the Blue Nile, and there's the evil Zionist soldier pouring water into Ethiopia, leaving just a few drops for parched Egypt.

The thing is, this didn't appear in a tinfoil-hat paranoid conspiracy website. This was the main editorial cartoon in *Al-Ahram*, one of Egypt's oldest mainstream newspapers, owned by the state itself.

Old habits die hard. It's an old habit to blame Israel for absolutely everything that goes wrong. It doesn't matter if it makes sense or not – whether, for example, the Mossad could really send a shark off the Egyptian coast to frighten tourists, or Israel would have anything to gain from selling poisoned seeds to farmers here. An expert called the way these Egyptians see Israel as a zero-sum game – if it's bad for Egypt, it must be good for Israel. And there's lots that's bad for Egypt these days.

An educated Egyptian tried to convince me that Israel was propping up the Islamist government of President Morsi from the Muslim Brotherhood. Pressed to explain the logic of that, considering the facts that the Brotherhood is dedicated, in theory, to Israel's destruction, and Israel has been warning of the consequences of Islamists taking over the region, he really couldn't come up with anything – except that he had concluded that the Morsi government was bad for Egypt, and therefore Israel must be behind it. Really.

What does this mean for relations, for the Israel-Egypt peace treaty? Probably not much.

All this wild speculation is just out there. People read it, some believe it, some talk about it, and then they go about their business. No one is marching on Jerusalem. They have much more important things to worry about. Not the least of them is the situation in the Sinai Desert.

There, Islamist militants are gaining strength and arrogance. One daring escapade was the abduction of seven Egyptian police officers and demanding release of prisoners in exchange for their freedom. The affair ended with a whimper after a week or so, and no one seems to know exactly what the militants got in return for the police.

But one result was a buildup of Egyptian military forces in the lawless desert. Under the peace treaty, that requires Israeli approval. There is no sign that Israel objected, because Israel has as much an interest as Egypt in bringing the jihadis in Sinai under control.

So as it has been for three decades, actual Israel-Egypt relations are guided by the interests of both countries, not wild conspiracy theories or satellite laser beams. That means cool on the surface, practical beneath it.

Under the present circumstances, that's the best we can do.

Chapter 36: Anti-Israel, but no big deal

"Israel no good."

The young taxi driver was smiling as he stated this obvious fact.

It's one of the most hackneyed clichés in journalism – the foreign correspondent fresh off the plane, interviewing his taxi driver so he'd have something to write about as soon as he checks in to his hotel.

It wasn't like that.

It was the other direction. We were driving to the airport through deserted Cairo streets early in the morning so I could catch a plane home.

I stopped the cab on the street outside my apartment and asked the driver to head to the airport. He was a typically friendly young Egyptian. We were just making conversation. His name was Sameer.

Sameer asked me where I'm from. I said Chicago. That's what I always say.

He responded the way everyone else here has. "Chicago? America?" Yes. "America good," he said. "Obama good."

Then, completely unprovoked, he added the rest.

"Israel no good."

Egyptians refer to the Israel-Egypt peace treaty as "Camp David." That's historically inaccurate. Camp David is where the two-part interim accords were signed in 1978. There was a framework for the Israel-Egypt treaty and a framework for solving the Palestinian problem. The first was implemented when Israel and Egypt signed their treaty in 1979.

Egypt assumed the next step would be peace between Israel and Palestine, and then peace between Israel and the rest of the Arab world.

It never got beyond phase one.

That left Egypt hanging out to dry. It had broken Arab ranks and made peace with Israel on its own. Egypt, the largest, proudest and most powerful Arab nation, was suspended from the Arab League, which had its headquarters in Cairo. Insult followed insult.

So people here began to believe Israel was the cause of all of Egypt's problems. Egypt blamed Israel for failure to close a deal with the Palestinians. It still does.

He probably doesn't call these cactus fruits sabras as Israelis do

A close examination of history will show plenty of evidence that the Palestinians were at least as much to blame as Israel for missing peace opportunities, but that's a different subject.

What's important here is the perception. Camp David was not fulfilled, and Camp David is the Egyptian concept of relations with Israel.

Running in parallel with all this was another perception – Israel was behind all the mischief in the Arab world.

By the 1980s, despotic Arab regimes were feeling the resentment of their peoples. The once opulent Arab societies had deteriorated into sick dictatorships with a fabulously and ostentatiously wealthy upper crust looking down on the downtrodden masses, who in turn were looking up with seething anger.

Leaders had to find a diversion. Lucky for them, there was Israel.

The wildest conspiracy theories blossomed, most with the Mossad at their center. Food shortages? Internal conflicts? Scandals? Bribes? Just blame the Mossad. When a shark appeared off the Egyptian coast and frightened tourists, it was sent by...you guessed it.

The Mossad did pull off some escapades that defied belief, but the credit it got for practically everything that went wrong in the region must have been seen as quite a compliment by those who were running the Israeli spy agency.

Conspiracy theories are an ingrained part of Arab culture. At a Cairo party, a young Egyptian on-air reporter for a prominent TV network bent my ear for more than an hour, explaining to me how this country actually works. It was one conspiracy theory after another. The military was behind this, the Muslim Brotherhood was behind that, they agreed to stage this incident, they colluded with heaven knows who else to make that happen. The reporter presented no evidence.

So when news broke of Islamist extremists killing sixteen Egyptian soldiers at the Gaza-Israel-Egypt border, stealing armored vehicles and crashing into Israel, I offered to bet an Egyptian colleague that within a day, Egyptian media would be full of theories blaming Israel. He didn't take the bet.

And sure enough, the next day, the Muslim Brotherhood itself charged that the Mossad was behind the attack. It was in all the papers. Evidence – Israel knew it was coming, ordered its people out of Sinai and warned Egypt, and Israeli forces stopped the terrorists before they could carry out an attack there. Aha.

How many people here actually believe this nonsense? It's hard to say.

Sameer, the taxi driver, would accept the Mossad conspiracy theory in the blink of an eye. Not because he's an evil person. Not because he actually hates Israel, any more than I "hate" eggplant.

Because that's just the way he's been brought up to think.

Chapter 37: Learning from the Bible

For a significant part of the year, the weekly Bible portions read in synagogues around the world take place in Egypt.

The Egypt that comes across in the story of Joseph is a nation that can easily feed itself, and with long-term planning, it can export to the rest of the region. It's a story of agriculture, governance and a bit of guile.

Until a few years ago, Egypt still exported wheat. Now Egypt is the largest importer of wheat in the world.

When Gamal Abdel Nasser took power here after the 1952 revolution that ousted the hated monarchy, he was acclaimed as a national savior and hero. Despite his record, he still is.

It's almost blasphemy to write something like this, but here's the truth: Egypt is still suffering from his policies, especially in agriculture.

Nasser seemed to have the right idea. He took farmland from quasi-feudal owners and distributed it among the people. He set up cooperatives to market their goods. His government told them all what to produce.

But Nasser's goal and its implementation were political – socialism, not efficiency – and soon it all broke down into chaos.

Experts say Nasser's goal was not to create a modern, profitable agriculture sector – rather, to provide cheap raw materials for Egyptian industry, like cotton for textiles. The farmers never benefited.

Today the cooperatives are gone, huge numbers of small farms dominate the sector, and it's every farmer for himself. They reject government advice, relating it to the despised control of the Nasser era.

Each grows whatever he thinks will sell for a profit. Yet because his resources are limited, so is his production. An American expert notes that California farmers get up to fifty-five tons of tomatoes an acre, while Egyptian farmers produce less than a third of that. Pilot projects in Egypt have raised the yield above California's, but it's hard to implement them on a large scale because there are so many little farms.

Not to go too heavy on the numbers, but 55 percent of Egypt's people depend on agriculture for their livelihood, yet they produce only 14 percent of the GDP. Egypt's wheat production peaked at 8.3 million tons in 2011, and it has to import another 5 million tons each year.

The reasons for this can be traced back to Nasser, except one. The region's population has quadrupled since 1960, when Nasser was in power.

Since then, as Nasser's misdirected system imploded under its own weight, governments have failed to reform the industry. Even positive efforts have foundered under bureaucracy and lack of planning.

Egypt is mostly desert, yet the Nile runs through the whole length of the country. That means converting desert land to farmland is not unrealistic. Efforts are well underway, but the convoluted process of purchasing and cultivating the land makes it impossible for most farmers and even most companies to make the attempt.

Egypt's vital Nile River

And then there's the subsidy bugaboo. As in other sectors, subsidies have distorted this market, too. Basic bread and wheat flour are subsidized so heavily that there's a lot of waste, even in a country where so many millions struggle for their daily bread. Even expensive, imported wheat ends up subsidized.

That's because even though Egypt is capable of producing enough wheat for itself, there are only half the needed number of silos – a case of poor planning.

Joseph didn't have that problem. According to the Bible story, he managed to store enough grain to supply the region during a seven-year famine.

Among those who came to buy from him were his brothers, the ones who sold him into slavery. It's one of the best-known stories in the Bible. One part involves his half-brother Judah appealing to him to release his younger half-brother, Benjamin.

Interrupting the Joseph story is the tale of how Judah's daughter-in-law fooled him with a disguise. Judah admitted that he fell for it, and that she proved herself "more righteous than I am."

Now Judah faced Joseph, the viceroy of Egypt, and begged for the life of his half-brother Benjamin. Joseph was pretending to be an Egyptian.

What isn't usually noticed about this scene appears obvious to me.

Joseph and Benjamin were full brothers. Judah, the half-brother, looked at one, looked at the other and recognized who that regal man in front of him really was. Judah's speech mentioned their aged father over and over, playing on the viceroy's emotions, and it worked. Joseph tearfully revealed his true identity. Judah was not going to be fooled a second time.

Now Egypt is in a transition. It elected an Islamist leadership. Economics were not its thing. The economy is the main factor that brought it down.

The military took over, pledging to call a new round of elections. Then perhaps it will be the turn of the other side, the more secular Egyptians. One of their leading lights is Hamdeen Sabahi, who somehow has gained the support of many liberals. He finished third among thirteen candidates in the first round of Egypt's presidential election in 2012.

"Somehow" because Sabahi is a Nasserist. He is a follower of the heroic president who saved and then ruined the country. Nasser's picture can still been seen in many places.

Nasser's image on a campaign poster in downtown Cairo

"Most people are too young to remember what he actually did," observed one expert.

The people chose Islamists the first time around. Next time the choice was between the military ruler, al-Sisi, and the candidate with old, failed policies in disguise, Sabahi.

Fooled once, Judah figured it out the second time. You could say that Egypt did, too. Sabahi got only about three percent of the vote.

Chapter 38: Not so fast

I'm writing this on Tisha B'Av, the ninth day of the Hebrew month of Av, the day every year that Jews mourn the destruction of the biblical Temples in Jerusalem.

A main element of Tisha B'Av is a twenty-five-hour fast. Like the one on Yom Kippur, it begins before sundown and ends the next day after sundown.

Similarly, the Muslim holy month of Ramadan features daily fasts that begin at sunrise and end at sundown. For the second year in a row, Ramadan coincides with Av. So the Tisha B'Av fast parallels the Ramadan fast for a day.

Living in a Muslim country brings out some similarities between Judaism and Islam. Halacha, Jewish religious law, and Sharia, Muslim religious law, are radically different. But the two words mean virtually the same thing – roughly, "the way."

When someone asks when Ramadan starts, an easy way to figure it out is to look at the Jewish calendar. Ramadan starts on Rosh Hodesh, the beginning of the Hebrew month, give or take a day. Both religions use the same lunar calendar.

The difference is that Jews add a "leap month" every few years to keep their holidays in the same seasons. Muslims don't. So Muslim holidays – and Ramadan – move "backward" about eleven days a year.

I can hear construction workers downstairs, swinging their heavy sledge hammers at the walls of a fast-food restaurant on the corner. Fast-food places close for the whole month – there's not a lot of business if no one is eating all day. So Ramadan is the best time for renovations.

Construction work in Ramadan heat

Best for business, maybe, but not for the workers.

These young men are engaged in tough physical labor in temperatures regularly reaching 40°C (that's 104°F in the U.S.), without eating or drinking for fourteen hours – the length of daytime this time of year.

If that's not a test of faith, I don't know what is.

Some Muslim clerics have ruled that workers can drink a bit if they must – but they have to make up the fast days some other time. In fact, you don't see Egyptians eating or drinking on the street during Ramadan. Even those who are not observant respect it in public.

In Israel, while many fast on Tisha B'Av, most don't. It's a normal work day for most Israelis, and even those observing the day of mourning to the letter are allowed to work in the afternoon.

Just like the men downstairs.

There's a yearly debate about Tisha B'Av. Now that there is a Jewish state, should we be mourning at all? After all, Israel is in nominal control of the holy sites in Jerusalem, though Jews are banned from praying on the site of the Temples for religious and security reasons.

The same debate plays itself out to no conclusion every year.

Certainly the destruction of the Temples was a tragedy of biblical proportions. The book of Lamentations, which is read in synagogues just after the start of the observance of Tisha B'Av, is heart-wrenching in its pure sorrow. The detailed description of the destruction that's read every Yom Kippur during the midday service is shocking, whether it's the third or thirtieth time you hear it.

King Solomon built the First Temple in all its splendor, a huge complex in Jerusalem with the Holy of Holies as its centerpiece. There lay the Ark of the Covenant, and inside that, the original tablets from Mount Sinai, according to Jewish belief. The High Priest entered the Holy of Holies only once a year – on Yom Kippur.

The main feature of the Temple was the sacrifice ritual, described in the Bible in bloody detail in the entire book of Leviticus. Cows, sheep, pigeons, flour and oil were sacrificed to the Almighty every day for a whole list of reasons.

The First Temple was destroyed by invading Babylonians in 586 B.C.E., and the Jews were scattered to the four winds.

They returned centuries later, and King Herod rebuilt the holy structure, the Second Temple. Yet the centerpiece, the Holy of Holies, was empty. The Ark had been lost. But the sacrifices were renewed in all their gore.

Then in 70 C.E., the Second Temple was destroyed by the Romans. Again the Jews were scattered. A few remained, and Rabbi Yohanan ben Zakai rescued the religion from oblivion by setting up a rabbinical academy, starting the transformation of Judaism from a Temple-centric, sacrifice-dominated religion to a universal one of prayer, scholarship, laws and ethics.

When Jews mourn the destruction of the Temple today, part of the ritual is to pray for its reconstruction. Jews pray for that every day. The trick is to understand those prayers in the context of present-day reality.

Here's my way.

We attribute the destruction of the First Temple to specific sins of the Jews of the day. We accept that God punished them by allowing the Temple to be destroyed.

Let's assume that reconstruction of the Temple by King Herod was also God's will, as was its destruction – again attributed to punishment for sins.

Yet the Holy of Holies was empty. That gives me pause for reflection.

The Second Temple, with all its gold, marble and magnificence, was little more than a place to conduct sacrifices.

God allowed the First Temple to be destroyed. It was rebuilt. Then he allowed the Second Temple to be destroyed. The sacrifices ended. Rabbinical Judaism replaced them and thrives to this day, more than two thousand years later.

Is there any doubt that if Judaism had continued to be all about the Temple and the sacrifices, it would not have survived? Are there any major religions of the past millennium that are focused on animal sacrifice?

By destroying the Temples, Israel's enemies forced Judaism to move into the modern era.

That must have been God's message. After all, He sent it twice.

Chapter 39: Egypt, Turkey and Israel

Viewed from Egypt, it's clear what Turkey is up to in the Middle East. For one thing, Israel is no more than a foil in Turkey's well-staged drama.

Once, Turkey was Israel's most prominent ally in the non-Arab Islamic world. Israel trumpeted that alliance, proud of the fact that it could maintain friendly economic and even military relations with a large Islamic nation like Turkey.

Now that's gone.

The natural reflex in Israel is to ask, "What did we do wrong?" and "What can we do to fix this?"

From Cairo, the answers look simple. "Nothing" and "nothing."

For the past decade, Turkey has been shifting its focus, its self-identity. If once Turkey aligned with the West, it is now aiming to be a Mideast power. The rise of the Muslim Brotherhood in Egypt gave this aim a major boost. Its fall was just as great a setback – but the goals remain in place.

Turkey is a NATO member, but it is not in the European Union. Its rejection by the EU, ostensibly over its Islamic orientation, triggered the shift. Since then, there have been several public, nasty spats between Turkey and NATO, tempered by some cooperation over the Syria crisis.

And all the while, Turkey has been aiming to bolster its image and standing in the Arab world.

There is one guaranteed method to achieve that: bash Israel. Turkish Prime Minister Recep Tayyeb Erdogan, just elected president, has become a master of the practice. His most celebrated ploy was to provoke Israel's only living Nobel Peace Prize laureate, President Shimon Peres, into a shouting match over Gaza, and then storm off the stage of the world economic summit in Davos. That was in January 2009.

The ugly saga of the *Mavi Marmara*, when Israeli forces boarded the Turkish ship headed for Gaza to break the Israeli blockade and killed nine activists, played into Erdogan's hand. So did the silly maneuver of Israel's then-deputy foreign minister, Danny Ayalon, publicly embarrassing the Turkish ambassador to Israel. Erdogan could not have scripted those incidents better himself.

As a result of his anti-Israel grandstanding, Erdogan is received as a hero all over the Arab world. Egyptians cheered and celebrated when he visited Cairo in November 2012.

But Turkey's act is not all for show.

In 2011 Turkey offered Egypt a $1 billion credit line, and Egypt gladly accepted. Its foreign currency reserves have plummeted below the danger line and any help is welcomed. Turkey has invested $1.5 billion in Egypt and pledges to increase that substantially.

The March 2013 edition of an Egyptian monthly magazine, *Business Today*, devoted its cover story to burgeoning Egypt-Turkey economic relations. The two countries have signed no fewer than twenty-seven trade agreements, and trade increased 30 percent in 2013.

Business Today's cover story was headlined, "Long Overdue Alliance." It focused on a retail trading concern expanding its business with Turkey, playing up the almost unlimited potential of the Egyptian consumer market. Overplaying, perhaps – while there are, indeed, more than eighty million people in Egypt, the World Bank says 40 percent live near or under the international poverty line of $2 a day, and they are not buying much from anyone.

The article listed five regional trading accords involving Egypt, the EU, Turkey, Africa, the United States and Arab nations. To illustrate, it showed this map:

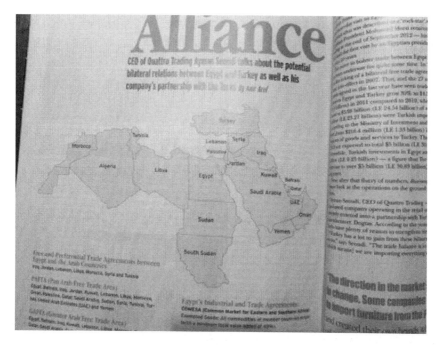

Not the whole story

Look what's missing. Not just "Israel." Also, an arrangement that has revolutionized Egyptian textile exports – the Qualifying Industrial Zones (QIZ) accord signed by Egypt, Israel and the U.S.

It allows Egypt to export its products customs-free to the U.S., as long as the products have 10.5 percent Israeli input. It's a bit more technical than that, but those are the bare bones.

The pact went into effect in 2005. Since then, more than seven hundred Egyptian companies have taken advantage of it, and they bring more than $1 billion a year into Egypt, according to the Egyptian government.

There was some speculation that the Muslim Brotherhood would try to cancel the deal when it took power here, but just the opposite – Egypt started negotiating with Israel to lower the Israeli component a bit. That amounted to an indirect endorsement of the pact.

That's because the Muslim Brotherhood is not suicidal. *Business Today*, in the same edition that printed that map, noted that the textile industry employs more Egyptians than any other manufacturing sector – no less than 30 percent of the work force. The QIZ is a crucial element in that. In 2012, the U.S. expanded it to include more Egyptian firms.

Responding to my question, the deputy managing editor of *Business Today* said the map was just an illustration of the nations that have free trade agreements with Egypt, and Israel doesn't. Without my asking, he said the QIZ pact isn't in that category.

QIZ has not been a factor in Egyptian government policy discussions since the military reassumed control. It continues to benefit Egypt, quietly and efficiently.

So Turkey gets the magazine cover, and on a larger scale, the public adulation. Turkey is the one making noise, much of it directed against Israel. For better or worse, that's the key to popularity in the Arab world. And that is Turkey's aim. Israel is just a means to the end.

That's why there is nothing Israel can do to improve relations, at least in public. An apology over the *Mavi Marmara* has not turned it around, since the Turkish goal is to use Israel as a way to fame and fortune in the Arab world. Even the eventual agreement that included the Israeli apology has not been implemented, ostensibly over a disagreement about the level of compensation to the families of the nine dead – another example of how far Israel is prepared to go to mollify its counterparts, and how far its counterparts are prepared to go to rebuff its offers.

What needs to be understood here is this: Just as there are two sides to the Israeli-Palestinian conflict, and not everything depends on what Israel does – there are two sides to the Israel-Turkey conflict, and not everything depends on what Israel does.

So the most beneficial policy for Israel would have been to sit back and do nothing. Do nothing to provoke, and do nothing to promote, at least in public. As with Egypt, there might be opportunities to develop relations behind the scenes, if they are in the best interests of both countries.

Like the QIZ. It works so well because it's the "peace treaty" no one has heard of.

Chapter 40: Israeli Spring

Viewed from Cairo, Israel's parliamentary election in January 2013 looked somehow familiar. It looked like Israeli Spring.

Yet the world continues to relate to Israel as if nothing has changed.

Reporters, analysts, diplomats and "experts" sat at their desks with their pencils – OK, with their computers, I guess I gave away my age – figuring out the blocs, who wants peace, who doesn't want peace.

But that isn't what actually took place as 3.5 million Israelis stood behind the rickety cardboard enclosures, contemplated nearly three dozen piles of slips of paper with different initials on each, picked one, put it in an envelope and dropped it into a plastic ballot box.

At least I assume that's how it worked. That's how it's been since 1973, when I voted for the first time. This was the first election since then that I missed, because I was in the "Diaspora," if you can call Cairo that. Israel doesn't allow absentee ballots for ordinary people like me.

For the first time since 1973, and probably before, Israelis didn't vote primarily about Palestinians. That's revolutionary.

Some did, of course. Benjamin Netanyahu's backers gave his Likud twenty seats of the 120 in parliament, and it's likely many of them voted for his stonewalling approach to peace negotiations. Another twelve went to Jewish Home, dedicated to the cause of the settlers and the biblical Jewish homeland where they live.

Perhaps some of those who gave Yisrael Beitenu eleven seats, running with the Likud, also voted on the classic Palestinian issue. More likely they had other things on their minds. The party's constituency is largely secular immigrants from the former Soviet Union, who are concerned about the economy and other domestic issues.

Yisrael Beitenu head Avigdor Lieberman acknowledged that approach when he counseled the prime minister to concentrate on local affairs, because trying to build a coalition around peace efforts would lead to deadlock. This from the man who had spent the previous four years as Israel's foreign minister.

The voting patterns of the other two-thirds of the electorate reveal the revolution even more clearly.

The ultra-Orthodox voted for their parties as they always do, striving to protect their special status. Likewise many Israeli Arabs.

That left the secular, more dovish electorate that used to vote as a bloc for parties that promised to bend over backwards for peace with the Palestinians.

They had two parties to choose from, old-time doctrinaire dovish Meretz and latecomer Hatnuah of former Foreign Minister Tzipi Livni, whose whole platform was making peace. Together they got all of twelve seats.

In contrast, two parties, one old and one new, took thirty-four seats while putting domestic issues like unacceptable and growing income gaps, housing prices and subsidies to ultra-Orthodox Jews at the top of their agendas. Their thirty-four seats are more than Likud-Beitenu won.

Yesh Atid was a new entry with a fresh slate and no history on the peacemaking front. When pressed, party leader Yair Lapid made the obligatory statements about the need for peace negotiations.

Then there's Labor, the home of peacemakers like Shimon Peres and Yitzhak Rabin. As peace efforts foundered, it sank lower and lower and disintegrated. New leader Shelly Yachimovich came along and completely changed its course. She adopted Israel's social protest movement and refused to be drawn out much about Palestinians. It was a huge gamble, and it appeared to have paid off in a relatively respectable showing.

So thirty-four seats for domestic issues. Probably more. Revolution. But almost no one outside Israel seemed to notice.

"Experts" dug around in the campaign statements of the candidates to ferret out how they feel about Palestinians. The "peace process" is the only issue to them. Even Labor turned on its new leader and reversed course a year after the election, selecting old-school pol Isaac Herzog to replace Yachimovich. Every second word out of Herzog's mouth is "Palestinians."

He and the pundits are missing what the Israeli people tried to tell them.

It's not as if the dovish voters suddenly don't want peace. Clearly they do. But many have given up on the process. There is a widespread feeling of frustration, that Israel has done whatever it could, made offers of far-reaching concessions for generous borders and arrangements for a Palestinian state, and nothing has come of it except more complaints, more charges, more demands, more insults – and especially, more rockets – from the Palestinian side.

There is a whole class of people in Israel known as "*meuchzavei Oslo*," meaning "let down by Oslo," referring to the Israeli-Palestinian peace process that started with secret talks in Norway in 1993. These were Israelis who strongly supported peace negotiations and the concessions Israel would have to make, believing that the final result would be peace between Israel and a Palestinian state next door.

It didn't work out that way. Responding to Israel's first offer in 2000, Palestinian leader Yasser Arafat walked away, and a violent uprising erupted, killing thousands. After the second offer, Palestinian leader Mahmoud Abbas walked away, and rockets rained down on Israel from Gaza again, which by then Abbas had lost to Hamas.

No wonder, then, that many Israelis feel let down by the process. These Israelis, who supported the peace process and still want peace with the Palestinians if that's possible, don't support Netanyahu's policy of angering the whole world with West Bank settlement construction. Most don't

215

support the settlements and wish they would go away. But they also don't hold out any hope for progress from further negotiations.

So they have turned inward to domestic affairs, hoping to fix their own society, distorted for so long by the obsession with the Palestinian issue.

They said that loud and clear on election day in January 2012, which was – poetically and unseasonably – warm and sunny.

Israeli Spring.

Time for the rest of us, from the Nile to the Thames to the Potomac, to put down our pencils and calculators and read the weather forecast.

Chapter 41: Opportunity, not burden

"Wow, you, Obama and Ronaldo at the same time," my son texted me on my arrival home from Cairo for the Passover holiday in March 2013.

I landed in the middle of the presidential visit, or "Obama-rama," as one colleague called it.

You might get the idea that President Barack Obama was the only subject anyone was talking about here. We reporters do tend to give the impression that the story we're covering is the only one there is. Three local TV stations gave the visit nonstop coverage.

Jerusalem was naturally obsessed with the visit, whether it wanted to be or not. At Cairo airport waiting to board our plane home, a colleague was weighing whether to try to get to his office in Jerusalem — whether there would be traffic jams, or perhaps people would be so cowed by the strict security measures that they would all stay home, and he could drive to his office easily. The verdict — there would be traffic jams. There always are. Jerusalem's streets are so narrow that traffic backs up in normal times, all the more so when main thoroughfares are closed down, even for short periods. It's why I buzzed around Jerusalem on a Vespa motor scooter for two decades on assignment.

Here in the Tel Aviv area, though, life went on. Radios and TVs were not blaring out Obama coverage from the shops and stores downtown. People seem more concerned with preparing for the approaching Passover holiday.

It's a holiday celebrating the exodus of the Israelites from Egypt, and the scriptures say pretty clearly that Jews are not supposed to return to Egypt.

So am I violating a religious commandment in the Imbaba souk in a Cairo slum next to the Nile, posing with my new friends – one a shopkeeper and the other, Mohammed Morsi, still president then?

Mark and friends in Imbaba

It takes some rabbinical contortions to get out of that, but I gave it a try around the Passover Seder table with family and friends. Some, especially my kids, were none too happy about it, but they agreed that I could go back to work in Egypt.

There are other things to try to make sense of in one of my infrequent trips home to Israel. The main one is the question of where this country is heading.

Inevitably the coverage of the Obama visit concentrated on the Israel-Palestine issue. Israel is said to be mistrustful of Obama, yet it gives him a warm welcome. If Obama is as harsh on Israel as Israelis believe, one would think that the Palestinians would have greeted him even more enthusiastically. Instead, they blocked roads, defaced and threw shoes at his posters, made threats and fired a rocket at Israel.

Obama agrees they deserve a state. Palestinians are angry he hasn't handed it to them. Chances are, given the inability of the two sides to finish a deal by themselves, that handing it to them – imposing a solution – is the only way they will get their state, but don't bet on dancing in the streets of Ramallah the next day when they don't get everything they want.

Israel, in the meantime, appears to be moving on to other issues, despairing of progress with the Palestinians after two serious attempts that nearly succeeded but crashed and burned in the end.

Israel's government has a new look and a new focus. It's turning inward, looking to resolve domestic issues. One of the main targets is the favors granted ultra-Orthodox Jews for decades.

This mission is described as "equal burden," a reference to drafting ultra-Orthodox men into the military. Tens of thousands of them get automatic exemptions to continue their religious studies in poverty, supported by tax money, while everyone else works and serves in the military.

Universal military service might have been a relevant issue nearly four decades ago, when I did basic training in the Israeli army. There were two ultra-Orthodox Israelis in my unit of mostly overage new immigrants. I remember Reb Avraham, a roly-poly, friendly, fortyish rabbi with a bushy black beard, dipping his breakfast coffee mug into the center of the huge vat holding the precious brown elixir, taking care not to touch the sides, as if that would make his coffee more kosher. It didn't, of course, but I could sympathize with a fellow coffee addict.

The rest of us treated them as just two other soldiers in the unit. We didn't question why they were there, and they didn't try to sway us to their religious point of view. That was in the mid-1970s, simpler times.

Even then, though, there was an undercurrent of resentment against their fellow ultra-Orthodox who took advantage of draft exemptions. The difference is – then the army needed everyone it could get. Today it doesn't.

Even if the government were able to ram through a draft of ultra-Orthodox men into the military, it would be a waste of time, effort and money. They are not qualified for most military positions, the army doesn't need them, and in candid moments, senior officers even say so in private.

Instead, Israel should be looking to bring most of them into society. Many would work if they had a chance, but not working is part of the no-army-service deal. Most of them are not cut out for the lives of cloistered academics, any more than most of the rest of us are. So they would benefit from studying secular educational subjects and getting work permits as much as the rest of society would benefit from not having to support them with welfare.

The key, according to a perceptive observer of Israeli society, sociologist Tami Lavie (my daughter), is to replace the mantra of "equal burden" with a slogan of "equal opportunity." Replace a negative with a positive, a goal to strive for instead of a penalty to impose.

In a larger sense, Israel has joined the rest of the region's spring. Like Egypt and the other countries, Israel found itself turning inward, trying to begin dealing with its domestic issues, instead of concentrating on foreign affairs and perceived external threats.

And like its neighbors, the efforts have not borne edible fruits in their first season.

It shows that in Israel, as in the rest of the Mideast, Arab Spring has to be seen as a concept, a long-term goal – not a quick fix. There will be more failures to live through, and the future is uncertain as always. Just as the problems are enormous, so is the potential.

Afterword: Going home

It's been so much more than I expected.

Working in Cairo off and on for four years, living here for the last two, has been like graduate school in political science.

I gained a new understanding of what the Mideast is, what Islam is, what the emerging world is, and where Israel fits into it all.

I've made friends, had some fun, explored one of the world's biggest and poorest cities, dodged cars on six-lane roads, navigated my way around in Arabic, become used to the muezzin at the mosque next door calling the people to prayer five times a day, watched two revolutions and two coups up close, experienced Arab Spring from Cairo. What a ride.

Now it's almost over.

There is much to ponder, much to remember. Pictures like this one, me mugging at the Roman-era Pompey's Pillar in Alexandria, will keep it real.

Pompey and me

I'm not much of a tourist, I admit. I look for interaction with people, contact with society, understanding of mindsets and politics more than recreational, historical and cultural attractions.

I come away with an insight that surprises me. I moved to Israel in 1972. For four decades I thought I was living in the Mideast. I was wrong.

Egypt is the dominant face of the Mideast – not Israel, not the wealthy Gulf.

My first lesson was the raised eyebrows I got when I asked a colleague where I should open a checking account. "This is a cash economy," he said. "Nobody takes checks." That fact has vast economic implications, none of them good.

My "checking account" became an ATM machine, where I took out piles of cash to pay for everything. After searching bank branches for one that would give me the amount set by my bank, I finally tried the little ATM next to the entrance of my apartment building, wedged between the fast food restaurant and the candy store, with no bank in sight. We've had a close, personal relationship ever since.

My personal bank

Another lesson came when I wanted to pay my rent a week early because I was going home on vacation. I told the doorman, Ahmed – he's a fiftyish, friendly, helpful fellow whose job is to keep this old building running. He went into the office and started fumbling with the receipt book. I figured they hadn't filled out the receipts yet, since it was early, so I opened the spiral pad I still carry in my pocket (gave away my age again), turned to a blank page and asked him just to write down a receipt there for the meantime.

He took the pad and the pen, hesitated, and laboriously scrawled his name. I had no idea that he's illiterate. I hope I didn't embarrass him.

Literacy here is only 71 percent, but younger Egyptians are more likely to be able to read and write than older ones. Ahmed's son, Mustafa, who's in his twenties, is literate. That, too, has significant implications for a nation struggling to become democratic.

As I walk through ordinary neighborhoods, people greet me with curiosity, because "tourists" don't usually appear there, or with friendliness – usually both.

Hassan the watchmaker charges me seventy-five cents to replace a broken watchband post and insists on bringing me a cup of tea. We share a pleasant few minutes in his tiny shop.

Sameer from the fruit and vegetable stall notices that I like the old, discontinued 25-piaster coins with holes in the middle. He saves me a few.

Replaced by ordinary coins

Abdul, the custodian at the office, is amused that I greet him every day in Arabic. His smile is always a nice start to my shift.

Of course, all this pleasantness is only part of the story.

I've never talked to the two men who sleep outside the door to my building. I think that's where they "live." Or the young woman who drags herself down the street on her knees, stopping to beg for a coin or two.

The poverty here is mind-numbing. The place where I live is described as an "upscale neighborhood." True, there are some foreign embassies here in beautiful buildings like this one, the Bahrain Embassy just down the street from my apartment house.

One face of my neighborhood

But most of the apartment buildings are like mine – old, a bit crumbling. So upscale is relative. There are slums in Cairo that make Palestinian refugee camps look upscale. Much of the housing in this population-exploding city is illegal – or informal, as they call it here. From time to time one of the informal apartment houses collapses, just like that.

The economy is the overriding crisis. Three years of political turmoil has only made it worse, though calm and stability, not constant demonstrations, are vital for fixing the economy. About 40 percent of Egypt's people live near or below the international poverty line of $2 a day per person. They survive because basic foods and fuel are heavily subsidized.

Everyone benefits from the subsidies, even people like me, earning a foreign income. Granted, I'm a legendary cheapskate, but I live on $1,000 a month here, including everything. So something's wrong.

And all the stories here are about men. Egyptian women don't interact with men. They keep their heads down. They are, as a rule, oppressed and harassed. Even women I know don't look at me unless I greet them first.

So I have learned unforgettable lessons in my two years of living here. The easiest, most superficial one is that Israel isn't so bad.

It's time to go home.

Epilogue

"Arab Spring is all about Israel" – a satire

"No, I think you should keep the president of Yemen there at least a couple more weeks, while we get things straightened out."

I could hear only one side of the conversation, but I think he was talking to someone in Saudi Arabia.

"You have to understand, this has to fit into the overall picture. It's all a matter of timing," he said, snuffing out yet another cigarette in a smoldering, overloaded ashtray. "I don't have all the Palestinian September ducks in a row yet, so I need to keep this boiling a while."

I can't give you his name. He didn't even give it to me. He says I have to call him Z. Otherwise this interview is over, and he implies a lot more than that will be over, too. He's already got my press card, and worse, my health insurance card.

I can tell you that his office is in the basement of the Israeli Defense Ministry, that top-secret, heavily guarded, camouflaged complex in the middle of Tel Aviv that is almost invisible, if you don't notice that 200-foot-high antenna thing right in the middle. It might as well have a bulls-eye on it, but I'm sure there's a sophisticated reason behind that. Here in Israel, and especially here in the defense establishment, there is always a sophisticated reason.

Israel's invisible Defense Ministry

Z is finally off the phone with, I think, Saudi Arabia. It's the fourth phone call he's taken since I was escorted in here, blindfolded and stripped naked, by four goonish security officers. At least I think there were four. I was blindfolded. And naked.

I had innocently made a phone call and asked to interview the guy who's running Arab Spring. Within minutes a jeep screeched to a halt in front of our office and a short guy with a typical Israeli military paunch got out, surrounded by four crew-cut, burly guys with earpieces, vests and bulges in the wrong places. The short guy looked vaguely familiar.

The entourage raced up the steps – well, raced might be a bit much, because the guy in the middle with the paunch doesn't race much anymore. What they did was more like run in place, so it looked like the important one was racing.

Eventually they got to my desk. "I'm sure you know who I am," the main dude said. I didn't, really. I've only been working here for three weeks, and usually I just do filing and cover boring archeology stories, and then they yell at me that they still spell archeology "archaeology," with an extra "a." Whatever.

A girl walked by. I think she's the bureau chief. Or chief photographer. Something like that. "That's Barak," she whispered. Barak. Barak. Damn. I know that name. Which one is that again? Prime minister? Defense minister? Mossad? The guy who runs the pharmacy downstairs?

I was getting a little nervous, but the guy lisped, "You have nothing to worry about. Israel is the only democracy in the Middle East." He quickly added, "Israel's army is the most moral army in the world." That made me feel a lot better.

So when they threw the burlap bag over me and dragged me away, I wasn't the least bit concerned. And when they stripped off my clothes in a dark room somewhere after a bumpy ride in that jeep, I assume it was just for my own good, because I had pissed my pants. Well, justifying it to myself, until a month ago I was writing obits in Toledo, and this kind of stuff never happens in Toledo.

"Why did you ask to interview the guy who runs Arab Spring?" asked the guy with the lisp, this Barak. By now I recognized his voice. He was the one who said twice on a live CNN interview that the Arab position was "all propaganda and bullshit." Twice. I still have the tape of that. I figured I better not try to bullshit him.

"Well, it's obvious that Israel is behind all this," I said carefully, "because we keep writing stories about how Israel comments on this, how Israel is worried about that, how the world should be scared to death of the third thing. So clearly Arab Spring is all about Israel."

"I can confirm that," said Barak. "But what about the interview request?"

"It's just logical that if this is so important to Israel, there must be one person who's in charge," I croaked, because the blindfold was so tight it was constricting my throat. "I just wanted to talk to him."

Barak turned to one of the guards and said, "This fellow obviously understands how this country works. We can trust him to do a proper interview with Z." At least that's what I think he said. I learned some Hebrew in Sunday school. I don't think he said, "This doofus doesn't have a clue. Let's take him to Z and scare the shit out of him."

They wrapped a towel around me before I went into Z's office, and they took off the blindfold, too. I was eternally grateful. Through the narrow window at the top of Z's basement room, I could see the base of the two-hundred-foot antenna tower, so I knew where I was.

Z lit another cigarette, squinted as the smoke wafted past his face, and fixed me with a bleary-eyed gaze.

"Where were we?"

Well, we weren't really anywhere, since he kept getting phone calls.

The phone rang again.

"Dammit, I told you a hundred times that these little demonstrations in Tahrir Square on Fridays are no problem," he bellowed. "Stop denouncing them. If you guys in the Brotherhood just lay back, all this will blow over and you can take over as we planned."

What? Israel is planning a Muslim Brotherhood takeover of Egypt?

I squeezed in the question.

"Of course that's Israel's plan," he shouted. "Were you born yesterday? Don't you hear Netanyahu warning at least twice a week that the Brotherhood is going to take over Egypt? Do you think he just makes warnings like that la-de-da and then nothing happens? As if we're not supplying Iran with nuclear weapons?"

I'm starting to get it now.

"And I suppose all you idiot journalists think that the fact that Egypt's election is set for September is some sort of cosmic coincidence? Do you have any idea how much work it took us to coordinate all this? First we had to burn that guy in Tunis. Then we had to set up Internet connections in Egypt. Then we had to turn them off and piss off the reformer pansies. Then we had to get Mubarak out safely. You want to see him later? He's down the hall."

"What's the thing about September," I asked.

Z rolled his eyes. "That's when the U.N. General Assembly session starts," he said, as if he was lecturing a ten-year-old. "That's when the Palestinians want to get recognition of their state."

I still wasn't exactly following.

"OK, let me spell it out for you in terms even a journalist can understand. We are all in favor of the U.N. General Assembly recognizing a Palestinian state. That will keep the Palestinians busy for years while we go about doing whatever the hell we want, as usual. What we need is a diversion, something to distract attention from the whole U.N. show so no one else notices."

Now it was becoming clear.

"So we started this thing that's called 'Arab Spring.' Arab Spring, my ass. Tunisia gets chaos, Egypt gets the Brotherhood, Libya keeps Gadhafi, Syria keeps Assad, and who cares what Yemen gets, as long as they do it in September. The Brotherhood taking over Egypt probably would have been enough, but you can never be too sure, so we organized the rest of it, too."

"And you're the guy who is behind all this?"

Z looked at me confidentially. "Yes. That's my job. So far we're doing pretty well, I'd say. We got Tunisia and Egypt going the right direction, Syria and Yemen falling apart, Gadhafi making an ass of himself and the Palestinians still thinking anyone cares about them with all this stuff going on around them. So yeah, this is working out pretty well for us, thanks to me."

He added, even though he didn't need to, "So you're right. 'Arab Spring' is all about Israel. Just as you fatheads have been writing over and over. You just got the reasons wrong."

Then he squinted through the curling smoke and made sure I was paying attention to his final quote for my interview:

"And if you write even one word about this, the only democracy in the Middle East will send the most moral army in the world to Toledo, and we might or might not let you say good-bye to your family there first."

Made in the USA
San Bernardino, CA
02 August 2018